DON WEEKES

HARDCORE
Hockey
TRIVIA

GREYSTONE BOOKS
Douglas & McIntyre Publishing Group
Vancouver/Toronto/Berkeley

For Sammy Lazarus—you made us all so proud.

Greystone Books
A division of Douglas & McIntyre Ltd.
2323 Quebec Street, Suite 201
Vancouver, British Columbia
Canada V5T 4S7
www.greystonebooks.com

Library and Archives Canada Cataloguing in Publication
Weekes, Don
    Hardcore hockey trivia / Don Weekes

    ISBN-13: 978-1-55365-061-4   ISBN-10: 1-55365-061-1

    1. National Hockey League—Miscellanea 2. Hockey—Miscellanea.
I. Title.

GV847.W367 2004   796.962′64   C2004-903126-0

Library of Congress Cataloging-in-Publication Data
Weekes, Don.
    Hardcore hockey trivia / Don Weekes.
    p. cm.
    ISBN-13: 978-1-55365-061-4   ISBN-10: 1-55365-061-1 (trade paper)
    1. Hockey—Miscellanea. I. Title.
GV847.W436 2004
796.962—DC22   2004052388

Editing by Christine Kondo
Cover design by Jessica Sullivan
Cover photo by Bruce Bennett
Interior design and typesetting by Lisa Hemingway
Printed and bound in Canada by Friesens
Distributed in the U.S. by Publishers Group West

We gratefully acknowledge the financial support of the Canada Council for the Arts, the British Columbia Arts Council, and the Government of Canada through the Book Publishing Industry Development Program (BPIDP) for our publishing activities.

DON WEEKES *is an award-winning television producer at* CTV *in Montreal. He has written numerous hockey trivia books, including co-authoring the* Unofficial Guide *series.*

Contents

1 SMASH-MOUTH TRIVIA   **1**

Answers   7
Game 1: Hockey Crossword 1   20

2 MAKING MILESTONES   **22**

Answers   26
Game 2: Lefties & Righties   35

3 THREE-RING CIRCUS   **36**

Answers   40
Game 3: Bench Boss Blues   48

4 AROUND THE CIRCUIT   **49**

Answers   54
Game 4: Magnetic Attractions   61

5 DROPPING THE BUCK   **62**

Answers   66
Game 5: Hockey Crossword 2   74

6 TRUE OR FALSE? 76

Answers 80
Game 6: Backup to the Greats 90

7 TEAMWORK 91

Answers 97
Game 7: Stanley Cup Captains 108

8 STANLEY CUP FEVER 110

Answers 114

SOLUTIONS TO GAMES 120

ACKNOWLEDGEMENTS 124

1

Smash-*M*outh Trivia

WE'RE NOT SURE it's a trend but 2003–04 saw a number of biting incidents by players in fights. In January, Atlanta's Marc Savard bit the glove of Toronto's Darcy Tucker during a scuffle; and later, the NHL's first Inuit player, Jordin Tootoo, allegedly bit Columbus forward Tyler Wright's right pinkie finger during a brawl. After the game Wright took aim at his combatant's Arctic heritage: "He's from way up north—that's how they eat up there, I guess," Wright said. "That's why I was snapping. What was I supposed to do when I guy is biting me." In this opening chapter, we sink our teeth into some general trivia and spit out a few digits (numbers that is) of our own.

Answers are on page 7

1.1   Who is Joe Hockey?
- A. An NHL publicity director
- B. A hockey trivia expert
- C. A man who knows nothing about hockey
- D. A party animal in a TV beer commercial

1.2   Which NHLer occasionally celebrates scoring a goal by smashing himself into the rink glass?
- A. Jordin Tootoo of the Nashville Predators
- B. Georges Laraque of the Edmonton Oilers
- C. Jonathan Cheechoo of the San Jose Sharks
- D. Tie Domi of the Toronto Maple Leafs

1.3 Which player tied the record for playing with the most NHL teams in 2003–04?

    A. Igor Ulanov of the Edmonton Oilers

    B. Jim McKenzie of the Nashville Predators

    C. Reid Simpson of the Pittsburgh Penguins

    D. Mike Sillinger of the St. Louis Blues

1.4 Which NHL city hosted the largest crowd to attend a league game?

    A. Detroit

    B. Edmonton

    C. Toronto

    D. Miami

1.5 What is the greatest number of points scored by two teammates in one game?

    A. 10 points

    B. 12 points

    C. 14 points

    D. 16 points

1.6 Who was the first former NHL player to serve as a caddie at the U.S. Open?

    A. Dan Quinn

    B. Wayne Gretzky

    C. Grant Fuhr

    D. Wayne Cashman

1.7 Who was the only NHLer to play for all five of the NHL's first chartered teams in 1917–18?

    A. Joe Malone

    B. Dave Ritchie

    C. Newsy Lalonde

    D. Georges Vezina

1.8 Which defenseman said of his chances to win the top defenseman award in 2003–04: "The only Norris I know is Chuck?"

A. Bryan McCabe of the Toronto Maple Leafs
B. Wade Redden of the Ottawa Senators
C. Kim Johnsson of the Philadelphia Flyers
D. Sheldon Souray of the Montreal Canadiens

1.9 Who is Ryan Malone?

A. The first hometown player for the Pittsburgh Penguins
B. The first hometown player for the Los Angeles Kings
C. The first hometown player for the Philadelphia Flyers
D. The first hometown player for the Buffalo Sabres

1.10 What does the word "Moo-lay" refer to on the shaft of the stick of Edmonton Oiler Ryan Smith?

A. His custom made shaft
B. His hairstyle
C. His pre-game routine
D. His penchant for milk

1.11 How many hours did it take to play the world's longest hockey game?

A. 103 hours
B. 133 hours
C. 173 hours
D. 203 hours

1.12 Which NHL general manager was ridiculed on a Web site devoted to getting him fired in 2003–04?

A. Glen Sather of the New York Rangers
B. Jim Rutherford of the Carolina Hurricanes
C. Ted Leonsis of the Washington Capitals
D. Mike Milbury of the New York Islanders

1.13   What is the greatest number of end changes recorded in one game?

A. Three end changes

B. Six end changes

C. Nine end changes

D. 12 end changes

1.14   What is the longest suspension handed to an NHLer for past drug use?

A. 20 games

B. 40 games

C. 60 games

D. 80 games

1.15   Which NHL captain got into a highly publicized fight with a teammate at practise in 2003–04?

A. Saku Koivu of the Montreal Canadiens

B. Chris Pronger of the St. Louis Blues

C. Markus Naslund of the Vancouver Canucks

D. Keith Primeau of the Philadelphia Flyers

1.16   When he was traded in March 2004, how many games did Brian Leetch need as a New York Ranger to beat Harry Howell's team record for most games?

A. One game

B. 11 games

C. 21 games

D. 31 games

1.17   What is the fewest number of NHL games played by a father-and-son duo?

A. Seven games

B. 37 games

C. 67 games

D. 97 games

1.18 What unusual NHL first did Syd Howe face after mistakenly serving a teammate's penalty in 1935?

A. He became the first player assessed a $500 fine
B. He became the first player stripped of his captaincy
C. He became the first player assessed a game misconduct
D. He became the first player penalized for such an action

1.19 What is longest time one individual has spent as a member of an NHL team?

A. 31 years
B. 41 years
C. 51 years
D. 61 years

1.20 How many decades did Gordie Howe play pro hockey?

A. Three decades
B. Four decades
C. Five decades
D. Six decades

1.21 Who recorded the lowest games-per-goals ratio in a career of 1,000 games or more?

A. Craig Ludwig
B. Jay Wells
C. Brad Marsh
D. Ken Daneyko

1.22 Who has the lowest games-per-points ratio in a career of 1,000 games or more?

A. Luke Richardson
B. Brad Marsh
C. Ken Daneyko
D. Craig Ludwig

1.23 During the 1970s which head coach bucked the trend of dressing in a suit and wore an athletic tracksuit behind the bench during NHL games?

A. Barclay Plager of the St. Louis Blues
B. Bob Pulford of the Chicago Blackhawks
C. Ron Stewart of the Los Angeles Kings
D. Jean-Guy Talbot of the New York Rangers

1.24 Who was Joe Turner?

A. A little-known goalie with a championship trophy named after him
B. A journeyman defenseman with an NHL goal-scoring record
C. A little-league referee who became an NHL president
D. A fourth-line centre who played backup goalie in more NHL games than any other forward

1.25 What is the last NHL season without a 100-point team (excluding the lockout year 1994–95)?

A. 1969–70
B. 1979–80
C. 1989–90
D. 1999–2000

1.26 Who is Peter Demers?

A. A French play-by-play announcer
B. The inventor of the net cam
C. The NHL's first goal judge
D. A long-time team trainer

1.27 What was the outdoor temperature at the Heritage Classic, the NHL's first outdoor game played at Edmonton's Commonwealth Stadium in November 2003?

A. 21-degrees Fahrenheit/minus-6 Celsius
B. 11-degrees Fahrenheit/minus-11 Celsius
C. Minus 1-degree Fahrenheit/minus-18 Celcius
D. Minus 11-degrees Fahrenheit/minus-24 Celsius

1.28 **What is the age of the oldest rookie coach?**
A. 53 years old
B. 56 years old
C. 59 years old
D. 62 years old

1.29 **Which professional hockey league was the first to mandate the use of protective visors for all of its players?**
A. The American Hockey League
B. The East Coast Hockey League
C. The United Hockey League
D. The Central Hockey League

1.30 **Considering that the NHL was formed in 1917–18, in what year did the last original NHL player retire?**
A. 1922–23
B. 1927–28
C. 1932–33
D. 1937–38

Smash-Mouth Trivia

Answers

1.1 **C. A man who knows nothing about hockey.**
Gordie Howe may have officially trademarked his nickname Mr. Hockey, but there is nothing he can do about Joe Hockey. In fact, Mr. Hockey, Joe that is, doesn't even know who Howe is. And he understands little about the made-in-Canada game. That's because Joe Hockey is Australian and there isn't much stick-and-puck culture in the land of kangaroos and crocodiles. Born to parents of Palestinian and Irish descent, the family name Hockedunian was anglicized Down Under. Ever since, he's been Joe Hockey. As a member for North Sydney in the Australian parliament and that country's Minister of Tourism

and Small Business, he's been to Canada but has no real sense of his name's power. "I've had Canadians try and buy my Web site," he said in a *National Post* story. "They always ring me up. When I registered joehockey.com, a Canadian offered me us$100,000 for [it]. I turned it down." That decision proved unwise, considering a hockey league now uses www.joe-hockey.com.

1.2 **B. Georges Laraque of the Edmonton Oilers.**

It's called the Laraque Leap and for anyone who hasn't witnessed his signature scoring celebration, watch out, especially if you're sitting in Section 132 or 134, in Rows 1, 2 or 3 at Edmonton's Rexall Place. Laraque doesn't just high-five, arm-pump or team hug, his form of celebration is pure smash-mouth hockey. After a big goal at home, almost always in the south end net, the six-foot-three, 245-pound Laraque freight-trains it into the glass, jumping up with arms wide apart and face grimaced. His chest slams the glass with a thunder and his knees pound the dasher between the glass and the boards. "I hit it as hard as I can. It hurts like crazy," said Laraque in the *Edmonton Journal*. Why does he do it? "Because it [scoring goals] doesn't happen so often, I go crazy. I have so much adrenaline that I have to release it. This is my way to release it," said Laraque.

1.3 **D. Mike Sillinger of the St. Louis Blues.**

In 2003–04 Sillinger joined the ranks of Michel Petit and Jean-Jacques Daigneault as the only players to suit up for a record 10 NHL teams. Petit's career ended in 1997–98 and Daigneault's in 2000–01. Given his age, 34 years, and apparent tradability, Sillinger could top both players. His journey started with Detroit in 1990–91, then moved on to Anaheim, Vancouver, Philadelphia, Tampa Bay, Florida, Ottawa, Columbus, Phoenix and St. Louis in 2003–04. During his career Sillinger has endured a league-record seven mid-season trades, including four consecutive spilt-seasons from 1997–98 to 2000–01. He played full seasons with only three teams: Detroit, Vancouver and Columbus, each club (like the other seven) finally giving up hope that the small but burly centre with the 20-goal hands might play two-way hockey and cut down his awful plus-minus numbers. New additions to the 10-team club could include Jim McKenzie and Reid Simpson, both on their ninth NHL team in 2003–04.

1.4   B. Edmonton.
The Heritage Classic at Edmonton's Commonwealth Stadium on November 22, 2003, established a few league marks, including the first outdoor game, the coldest match ever played and the largest crowd in attendance. Huddled in thick winter coats, hats, scarfs, mitts and even snowmobile suits, the crowd of 57,167 more than doubled the previous NHL high of 27,227 fans, who watched Florida beat Tampa Bay 2–0 in the warmer confines of St. Petersburg's Thunderdome on October 9, 1993. In Edmonton, on chippy ice, Montreal beat the Oilers 4–3.

1.5   D. 16 points.
On February 20, 1981, Peter and Anton Stastny both counted hat tricks for the Quebec Nordiques in a 9–3 romp over Vancouver. Two nights later, the Slovak duo ran wild against Washington, as Peter counted four goals and four assists and Anton added three goals and five assists in an 11–7 win. Not only did the Statsnys establish a new record for most points by two brothers in a game, they also set a new NHL mark for most points by two teammates.

1.6   A. Dan Quinn.
After retiring from hockey in 1996, Quinn devoted himself to golf and became a major player on the Celebrity Tour. At the 2000 U.S. Open at Pebble Beach, when John Daly's regular caddie had to withdraw with a bad ankle, Quinn was enlisted as

his replacement. He got a close-up look at one of Daly's infamous meltdowns on the 17th hole as the golfer smacked one shot into a backyard and deposited three others into the Pacific Ocean. After carding a 14 on the par-5, Daly stormed off the course in disgust.

1.7   B. Dave Ritchie.
Ritchie was the only player to don sweaters with all five original NHL clubs. When the league began in 1917–18, Ritchie's rights were owned by the Quebec Bulldogs. Since Quebec did not ice a team that year, he joined the Montreal Wanderers for four games, before they withdrew from the league. The Ottawa Senators picked up Ritchie for the remaining 14 games of 1917–18. During the next several years the defenseman played with the Toronto Arenas, Quebec and the Montreal Canadiens, where he ended his career in 1925–26.

1.8   D. Sheldon Souray of the Montreal Canadiens.
After breaking Montreal's team record for single-game points by a defenseman in an 8–0 whitewash against the anemic Pittsburgh Penguins on January 10, 2004, Souray kept scoring points with his self-deprecating sense of humour during the post-game interviews. Besides his Norris wisecrack, Souray, who scored once and added five assists to break the Canadiens record of five points held by the great Doug Harvey and Lyle Odelein, also quipped: "The only Harvey they've ever associated me with is the place you build your own burger."

1.9   A. The first hometown player for the Pittsburgh Penguins.
Malone, a fourth round pick in 1999, became the first Pittsburgh born-and-trained player to suit up for the Penguins in 2003–04. He is also the first native Pittsburgher to reach the NHL, 36 years after the team joined the league in 1967–68. Malone was fourth among rookies with 22 goals and 44 points,

the best freshman goal count by a Penguin since Shawn McEachern in 1992–93. Malone wore the same No. 12 as his father, Greg, wore with the Penguins. Greg Malone is the team's head scout.

1.10   **B. His hairstyle.**

Smith is the only player in NHL history to score all the goals by both teams in one game on two occasions, scoring hat tricks in 3–0 wins on March 13, 2000, and November 14, 2000. Smith's custom made shafts from Hespeler feature a maple leaf, his late grandmother's initials and the word "Moo-lay," which his teammates jokingly use to pronounce "mullet," his coif of choice.

1.11   **D. 203 hours.**

Ever since a bunch of guys from Nova Scotia played 30 hours of hockey without a break and set the world record for the longest hockey game, there has been an epidemic of marathon games to get into the *Guinness Book of World Records*. After breaking the previous mark of 19 hours, eight minutes and 44 seconds set by record-holders in Red Deer, Alberta, the Nova Scotian's 30-hour game on January 5, 2002, was topped by other groups in Alberta, Saskatchewan and Ontario. In February 2003, a world-record 62-hour match was bested by an 80-hour game. Both records were dwarfed by another match in October 2003, which lasted 130 hours and seven minutes. Then, in April 2004, came word that two different groups in Sudbury, Ontario, were vying to set new records with 197-hour and 203-hour games. These 200-hour games were played with 40 players dressed in full equipment, in one- to three-hour long shifts under NHL rules on an indoor rink. They played for eight straight days. Any takers?

1.12   A. Glen Sather of the New York Rangers.
New York fans are not to be trifled with, especially when one
of their beloved sports teams, say the Rangers, suck. It can get
real ugly when things go wrong at Madison Square Garden.
Just ask Sather, who was brought aboard in June 2000 to turn
the club into a winner but instead was chased from his self-
appointed coaching position by chants of "Fire Sather! Fire
Sather!" at MSG in 2003–04. Disgruntled fans, who had not
seen their team in playoff form for six (going on) seven
seasons, also masterminded www.glensathersucks.com, a dev-
astatingly clever Web site dedicated to ousting Sather from his
New York job, listing in excruciating detail his failures as both
coach and GM. The site boasts a petition to have Sather fired, a
message board (Glen Sather is an idiot. Discuss.) and an audio
file to listen to an actual "Fire Sather" chant from the Garden.
Most damming is the meticulously researched list of personnel moves made during his tenure that depleted "the Rangers'
organization of quality young prospects through trades for
older veteran players."

1.13   B. Six end changes.
Instead of changing ends the customary three times, the
Boston Bruins and the St. Louis Eagles switched every 10 min-
utes during a game on January 15, 1935. The reason? A patch of
the rink at the east end of Boston Garden refused to freeze.
The spot was covered with a rubber mat. Boston won 5–3.

1.14   C. 60 games.
On September 27, 1990, the NHL suspended Edmonton goalie
Grant Fuhr for one year after he admitted to using cocaine ear-
lier in his career. In an August 31, 1990, interview with the
Edmonton Journal, Fuhr revealed that he had been using "the
substance" (he never used the word cocaine) since 1983 or
1984, and had used it on binges once every three or four
weeks. He also admitted that he had repeatedly lied to Oilers

GM Glen Sather about his drug use. The problem had gotten serious enough that Fuhr began receiving phone calls from angry drug dealers demanding payment. Fuhr's suspension was later reduced, allowing him to return after Edmonton's 60th game of the 1990–91 season. In his first game back, he blanked the New Jersey Devils 4–0.

1.15   A. Saku Koivu of the Montreal Canadiens.

Fights among teammates at practise aren't uncommon, but they are rare for team captains, the on-ice leader and player representative to management. Even more unusual is that captain, who had two stick altercations during a March practise, would be Koivu, the elite Finnish sharpshooter better known for his heroic fight against cancer than any other on-ice battle. Koivu's challenger was Mike Ribeiro, the 23-year-old Montreal native and team leader in scoring. Unlike other NHL cities where the press seldom attends practise, in Montreal, the media not only had footage, but they turned the skirmish into a full-blown Quebec language issue that dominated the front pages of all four Montreal dailies. French media criticized Koivu while their English counterparts rallied behind him. Worse, at the next home game boos rained down from the Bell Centre rafters when Koivu stepped on the ice. At the heart of the issue is something facing every Montreal captain: can he lead the Canadiens back to glory?

1.16   D. 31 games.

It's impossible to estimate the loss of Brian Leetch to the Rangers (or to New York City as a sports icon for more than a decade) but as Mark Messier observed the team "bottomed out" with his best friend's trade. As a lifetime Ranger, the Conn Smythe Trophy-winning Leetch had experienced everything that's wonderful about the game but also some of its misery, from the Stanley Cup highs of 1994 to six desperate seasons missing the playoffs. Leetch, the seventh-highest scoring defenseman in NHL history, played 1,129 games as a Blueshirt, just 31 short of old-time rearguard Harry Howell's team record of 1,160. His trade signalled the end of an era at Madison Square Garden. It came on his birthday, March 3, 2004.

1.17 A. Seven games.

Centre Bucky Buchanan laced them up for two games with the Rangers in 1948–49. His son Ron, also a centre, played three games with Boston in 1966–67 and two with St. Louis in 1969–70. Neither Buchanan got on the scoresheet during their NHL careers.

1.18 D. He became the first player penalized for such an action.

During a November 24, 1935, game against Toronto, Red Wings rearguard Ralph Bowman was given a minor penalty, but teammate Syd Howe mistakenly went to the box instead. After the penalty expired, the Leafs complained that the wrong Detroit player had served it. The referee agreed and assessed Howe a minor, the first time another player was penalized for serving a teammate's penalty. Detroit's Wally Kilrea protested the call and was assessed a misconduct for his trouble. Despite the gaffe, Detroit won 2–1.

1.19 D. 61 years.

The classic rink rat, Wally Crossman became a fixture at the Detroit Olympia when it opened in 1927. He worked as a soda jerk at a neighbourhood drugstore, sat in the balcony watching games for 25 cents and attended practises for free. In 1940, Red Wings GM Jack Adams hired Crossman as the club's dressing room attendant. He held the job for 61 years. In that time he saw 23 coaches come and go, had a ring-side seat for seven Cup championships and got his name inscribed on the Cup four times. In all that time he was never paid. He taped sticks, cut oranges for the players to snack on between periods, did the laundry and opened and shut the door on the bench during games in return for two free tickets to each game and tips from the players. Crossman finally retired after the 2000–01 season at age 90. "I've smelled enough sweat," he said. "I don't want to stay here until I'm 100. That's too long." Crossman died on January 29, 2003, at age 92.

1.20 D. Six decades.

Gordie Howe really didn't need to do this. On October 3, 1997, the 69-year-old grandfather signed a one-game contract with the Detroit Vipers of the International Hockey League in order to set a record that no one could topple: the only hockey player to appear in pro games in six decades. Howe started the game at right wing and did not wear a helmet. He played one shift of 47 seconds and did not touch the puck. Perhaps the most unsettling image of the entire escapade was seeing Mr. Hockey skate onto the ice through an inflated green snake head that was hissing fog. Howe's career began in 1946–47.

1.21 C. Brad Marsh.

Poster boy for scoring he's not, but Marsh read the defense very well and earned his keep playing stay-at-home hockey for more than 1,000 games. Marsh scored one goal every 47.2 games, just 23 goals in 1,086 matches from 1978–79 to 1992–93.

Lowest goals-per-game average in NHL history*

PLAYER	SEASONS	GOALS	GAMES	RATIO
Brad Marsh	1978–1993	23	1,086	47.2
Luke Richardson	1987–2004	32	1,247	39.0
Ken Dayenko	1983–2003	36	1,283	35.6
Craig Ludwig	1982–2000	38	1,256	33.1
Marc Bergevin	1984–2004	36	1,191	33.1

Current to 2003–04

Compared to Marsh, Luke Richardson and Ken Daneyko were red-hot snipers. Richardson ranks second, averaging one goal every 39 games and Daneyko ranks third with one goal every 35.6 games.

1.22 C. Ken Daneyko.

Brad Marsh and Craig Ludwig wear this record with pride, as they should. Each stuck to the blueline, netting only a point every five or more games, among the lowest in NHL history. Ludwig scored a point every 5.7 games (222 points in 1,256 games) and Marsh scored a point every 5.4 games (on 198 points in 1,086 games). But Daneyko has everyone in his dust with a scorching 7.2 games per point or 178 points in 1,283 games. Pulling up fast in second place is Luke Richardson with 7.0 (179 points in 1,247 games); and in third is Marc Bergevin with 6.6 (181 points in 1,191 games).

1.23 D. Jean-Guy Talbot of the New York Rangers.

Talbot only coached the Rangers for one season, but more memorable than his win and loss record was his game attire: a sweatsuit and turtleneck. His dress for success look drew few raves in fashion-conscious New York. His players weren't impressed either, finishing 1977–78 with a 30–37–13 before losing the preliminary round of the playoffs. "I wore a sweatsuit because it was a job and I sweat," Talbot said in a *Montreal Gazette* story. "Look at baseball and football coaches. They don't wear a shirt and tie."

1.24 A. A little-known goalie with a championship trophy named after him.

Joe Turner may be the goaltending fraternity's most famous one-game wonder. While more than 70 goalies have NHL careers of a single game, Turner stands out, not because of his 3–3 tie against Toronto after replacing an injured Johnny Mowers in the Detroit net on February 5, 1942, but because his story champions the heroics of all minor-league goalies who had little chance of ever making it to the big time. After his NHL debut, the Canadian-born Turner joined the U.S. Marine Corps to fight overseas. Unfortunately, he was killed in action in January 1945. As a tribute, the new IHL named its championship trophy after him. The Turner Cup was presented annually to the playoff winners until the league folded in 2001.

1.25 A. 1969–70.
Since expansion in 1967 only two seasons failed to produce a 100-point club: 1967–68 when Montreal led with 94 points and 1969–70, when Boston and Chicago tied for first place with 99 points.

1.26 D. A long-time team trainer.
Peter Demers is one of the longest-serving trainers in NHL hockey. In 2003–04, Demers, at 60 years old, was in his 32nd year treating the walking wounded of the Los Angeles Kings. He has massaged, iced, stitched up and stroked the egos of everyone from Marcel Dionne to Wayne Gretzky to Ziggy Palffy, working more than 2,500 games. Although to get a dressing-room story from him about a player would be breaking the trainer's code of silence, he reveals a lighter moment on the very serious subject of concussions, during the era of helmetless players: "But the joke going around was, you'd hold up three fingers and ask the guy 'How many fingers?' If he said 'two' or 'four,' you'd say: 'Close enough,'" said Demers.

1.27 C. Minus 1-degree Fahrenheit/minus-18 Celcius.
More than a game, more than a reunion, the Heritage Classic had all the boyhood wonder and magic of a pick-up game on a frozen pond under a crisp winter sky. There they were larger than life, Wayne Gretzky, Guy Lafleur and Mark Messier, Hall of Fame thirty and fourty-somethings taking turns at the time-

honoured tradition of shoveling snow from the outdoor rink built on the football field of Commonwealth Stadium. A hockey first for the NHL, 57,167 fans filled the stands to watch two games—the old-timer Megastars match and then the Montreal-Edmonton tilt—in sub-zero temperatures, and from a distance that reduced the players to ant-size proportions. Few came dressed to make a fashion statement, but they all had an opinion about the temperature: Freakin' c-c-cold. Montreal goalie Jose Theodore may have had the best idea, his Canadiens pom-pom toque was duck-taped to the top of his goalie mask. For the fun of it, Edmonton's old-timers beat Montreal's greybeards 2–0; and, for two points, the Canadiens won 4–3 over the Oilers. Gretzky's daughter, Paulina, sang the national anthem.

1.28   C. 59 years old.

Scotty Bowman, 69 years old, was the oldest coach in NHL history, but among rookies, Bill Dineen gets the golden cane, just a few years away from old-age security payments at 59 when he took over the demands of the Philadelphia Flyers in 1991–92. Dineen was born on September 18, 1932. He played five NHL seasons, including two with the Stanley Cup-winning Detroit Red Wings during the 1950s. Toronto great George Armstrong was 58 when he was handed the reigns of the Maple Leafs for one season, 1988–89. Among rookie coaches who never played in the NHL, John Brophy was 53 in his first season with Toronto in 1986–87 (just two years before Armstrong got the job), as was Steve Stirling, the New York Islanders coach of 2003–04. George Kingston was 52 with San Jose in 1991–92.

1.29 **B. The East Coast Hockey League.**

The ECHL pioneered pro hockey's first visor rule in 2003–04. The 31-team, class AA league, which has affiliations with 21 NHL clubs, may eventually change the face of hockey but their motivation came in part from ECHL teams trying to keep an eye on insurance premiums. Wayne Gretzky endorsed the league's decision to mandate eye protection, which, in place decades ago throughout hockey, might have reduced the 1,914 hockey-related eye injuries reported between 1972–73 and 2001–02. While the facts are chilling—311 players legally blinded in one eye, 302 of those suffered by players not wearing visors—it still doesn't change the opinion of some players, such as Peoria's Tyler Rennette. A 42-goal scorer and arguably the ECHL's top forward, Rennette goes through six half-shields per season. "I've always worn one, and I'm not taking it off," said Rennette in a *Peoria Journal Star* story. "But it's not right to tell pros they have to do this."

1.30 **C. 1932–33.**

A winner of three Stanley Cups, Reg Noble began his pro hockey career as a centre with the Toronto Blueshirts in the National Hockey Association in 1916, then joined the Toronto Arenas for the NHL's inaugural season in 1917–18, where he teamed with Babe Dye and Corbett Denneny to form the best line in the league. Moved back to defense in 1923–24, Noble went on to play 510 NHL games with the Arenas, St. Pats, Maroons, Cougars, Falcons and Red Wings, before retiring after the 1932–33 season.

Hockey Crossword I

ACROSS

1. Anaheim team
8. Broadcaster Dick _____
10. 1980s Boston tough guy Chris _____
12. Philadelphia's John _____ Clair
13. Full name of Russian sniper w. Atlanta
17. Crowd or _____ the goalie
18. _____ Belfour
19. Best pro hockey league
20. Montreal university, site of very first hockey game
22. Coast-_____-coast
24. Goalie Garth _____
26. _____ your words
28. 2000 Devil Cup winner, Jason _____
29. Mark on face
30. _____ Nedved
32. _____ Modano
33. Put the puck _____ _____
35. Oiler GM Kevin _____
38. Emergency Room, abbrv.
39. _____-timers game
41. Pittsburgh Cup winner Peter _____

42. Edmonton's _____ Smyth
44. Toronto's Owen _____
45. Montreal 1986 Cup winner Stephane _____

DOWN

1. _____ Wild
2. Long-time Hurricane Martin _____
3. Full name of long-time Chicago sniper
4. Montreal old-timer _____ Moore
5. Los Angeles D-man Joe _____
6. Veteran centre w. 10 teams, Columbus in 2002–03, Mike _____
7. Television, abbrv.
9. Philadelphia sniper Mark _____
11. & 20. Full name of St. Louis D-man w. hardest shot
14. Old-time Ranger from 1930s and 1940s, Ott _____
15. 1970s goalie _____ Dryden
21. Home of the Kings, abbrv.

23. Long-time Bruin Terry _____

24. Vancouver D-man Brent _____

25. Home town of the Senators

27. 1970s and 1980s Islander sniper Bryan _____

31. Dallas forward _____ Lehtinen

34. Brother of the Rocket, _____ Richard

37. Bruin old-timer from 1940, Pat _____

39. Bobby _____

40. Predators D-man _____ Hamhuis

43. Number, abbrv.

Solutions are on page 120

2

Making **M**ilestones

DURING GORDIE HOWE'S last season in 1979–80, two special 18-year-old rookies were beginning their NHL careers. Through the years they amassed goals and points that set numerous scoring records before finally surpassing Howe's feat of 1,850 career points. Wayne Gretzky and Mark Messier are the only players to top Howe's famous scoring milestone. In this chapter, we check out some milestone men in the making.

Answers are on page 26

2.1 Who is the youngest player in NHL history to lead or share the lead in goals in one season?

A. Charlie Conacher in 1930–31
B. Bobby Hull in 1959–60
C. Wayne Gretzky in 1981–82
D. Rick Nash in 2003–04

2.2 Which NHLer owns the league record for most overtime penalty shots?

A. Patrik Elias of the New Jersey Devils
B. Pavel Bure of the New York Rangers
C. Markus Naslund of the Vancouver Canucks
D. Peter Forsberg of the Colorado Avalanche

2.3 Why did Brett Hull change his jersey number and wear No. 80 at the start of 2003–04?

A. To honour a scoring legend
B. To honour a coach
C. To honour his father, Bobby Hull
D. To honour a scoring record

2.4 Who recorded the highest average of ice time among forwards since the statistic was introduced in 1998–99?

A. Pavel Bure of the Florida Panthers
B. Jaromir Jagr of the Pittsburgh Penguins
C. Joe Sakic of the Colorado Avalanche
D. Ilya Kovalchuk of the Atlanta Thrashers

2.5 In what season did an NHLer first play more games than the regular-season schedule?

A. During the NHL's 30-game schedule of 1924–25
B. During the NHL's 48-game schedule of 1934–35
C. During the NHL's 50-game schedule of 1944–45
D. During the NHL's 70-game schedule of 1954–55

2.6 Prior to Martin St. Louis and his league-leading 94 points in 2003–04, who was the last NHL scoring leader to record fewer points and win the title?

A. Gordie Howe in 1962–63
B. Stan Mikita in 1967–68
C. Jaromir Jagr in 1999–2000
D. Jarome Iginla in 2001–02

2.7 In 2002–03, referees used the video goal judge 214 times to review if the puck entered the net or not. How many goals were allowed compared to those disallowed?

A. 84 goals allowed; 130 disallowed
B. 104 goals allowed; 110 disallowed
C. 124 goals allowed; 90 disallowed
D. 144 goals allowed; 70 disallowed

2.8 Who became the youngest player in NHL history to score on a penalty shot in 2003–04?

A. Nathan Horton of the Florida Panthers

B. Michael Ryder of the Montreal Canadiens

C. Trent Hunter of the New York Islanders

D. Tuomo Ruutu of the Chicago Blackhawks

2.9 What is the NHL record for fewest days between penalty shot goals?

A. One day

B. Eight days

C. 16 days

D. 32 days

2.10 What is the greatest number of consecutive game-winning goals scored by a player from the start of his career?

A. Two straight game-winners

B. Three straight game-winners

C. Four straight game-winners

D. Five straight game-winners

2.11 Prior to 2003–04 when three players shared the NHL goal-scoring lead with 41 goals, when was the last time a player scored fewer goals to lead the league?

A. In 1958–59 when Jean Béliveau was goal leader

B. In 1962–63 when Gordie Howe was goal leader

C. In 1964–65 when Norm Ullman was goal leader

D. In 1967–68 when Bobby Hull was goal leader

2.12 How many defensemen rank among the top 10 all-time American-born NHL point leaders?

A. Two defensemen

B. Three defensemen

C. Four defensemen

D. Five defensemen

2.13 What is the highest goals-to-assists differential by a player in one season?

A. A differential of 21
B. A differential of 31
C. A differential of 41
D. A differential of 51

2.14 Which old-time sniper asked the league to take back a point from a January 1943 game total because he didn't believe he deserved it? At the end of the season, he missed winning the NHL scoring race by one point.

A. Lynn Patrick of the New York Rangers
B. Doug Bentley of the Chicago Blackhawks
C. Bill Cowley of the Boston Bruins
D. Billy Taylor of the Toronto Maple Leafs

2.15 What did rookie defenseman Thomas Pock accomplish in his first game with the New York Rangers in 2003–04?

A. He scored a goal
B. He scored a goal into his own net
C. He scored a goal that was called back
D. He scored a goal that was awarded to another player

2.16 Who was the first NHLer named Offensive Player of the Month in consecutive months since Wayne Gretzky last did it in 1986–87?

A. Mario Lemieux in 1988–89
B. Eric Lindros in 1994–95
C. Peter Forsberg in 2002–03
D. Martin St. Louis in 2003–04

2.17 What is the Gordie Howe hat trick?

A. Three goals in a game
B. Three consecutive goals in a game
C. A goal, an assist and a fight in a game
D. A two-, a five- and a 10-minute penalty in a game

2.18 What is the greatest number of shorthand points scored by a player in one game?

A. Three shorthand points
B. Four shorthand points
C. Five shorthand points
D. Six shorthand points

2.19 What is the greatest number of five-goal games by players in one season?

A. Two five-goal games
B. Three five-goal games
C. Four five-goal games
D. Five five-goal games

2.20 In November 2003 *Hockey Night in Canada* announcer Don Cherry called which Canadian junior star a "hot dog" because of the way he celebrated scoring a goal?

A. Corey Locke of the Ottawa 67s
B. Jeremy Williams of the Swift Current Broncos
C. Sidney Crosby of the Rimouski Oceanic
D. Corey Perry of the London Knights

Making Milestones

Answers

2.1 **D. Rick Nash in 2003–04.**
While everyone was watching Atlanta's sniper Ilya Kovalchuk tear up the league, Rick Nash was finding his NHL legs in Columbus, developing a reputation as a young gun who would charge the net and pay a price for goals. Along with Jarome Iginla, the threesome tied for the goal-scoring title with 41 goals in 2003–04, but Nash was still a teenager (a good excuse for his wild minus-35), the first in league history to win or share the goal lead.

Youngest goal-scoring leaders*

PLAYER	TEAM	SEASON	GOALS	AGE
Rick Nash	Columbus	2003–04	41	19 yrs., 293 days
Charlie Conacher	Toronto	1930–31	31	20 yrs., 92 days
Ilya Kovalchuk	Atlanta	2003–04	41	20 yrs., 354 days
Wayne Gretzky	Edmonton	1981–82	92	21 yrs., 68 days
Bobby Hull	Chicago	1959–60	39	21 yrs., 77 days
Charlie Conacher	Toronto	1931–32	34	21 yrs., 93 days
Wayne Gretzky	Edmonton	1982–83	71	22 yrs., 67 days

*From Elias Sports Bureau/*Current to 2003–04*

2.2   A. Patrik Elias of the New Jersey Devils.

Few players have ever been awarded penalty shots in overtime but Elias has two, both unsuccessful and both against the New York Islanders. He missed his first shot in a scoreless tie on December 1, 2000, against John Vanbiesbrouck; and his record-setting second opportunity in an extra period came opposite Garth Snow on December 10, 2003, in a 1–0 win. As of 2003–04, Elias has one other penalty shot, a goal against Damian Rhodes in a 9–0 win on March 10, 2000.

2.3   B. To honour a coach.

Hull, who wore No. 17 with Detroit, switched to No. 80 for the 2003–04 preseason to honour the late Herb Brooks, coach of the "Miracle on Ice" team that won the Olympic gold medal at Lake Placid in 1980. It is not without irony that Hull, known throughout his illustrious career as a coach killer, would pay tribute to Brooks. In fact, Brooks was the only coach Hull publicly admired, probably because both men wanted to give the game back to those who played it instead of those technicians who overcoached it. Hull played for Brooks during the two-week period of the 2002 Olympics. Brooks died in August 2003 at age 66 after falling asleep behind the wheel of his van on a Minnesota highway.

2.4 **A. Pavel Bure of the Florida Panthers.**
"Energizer Bunny" defensemen such as Chris Pronger and Nicklas Lidstrom routinely average 27 minutes per game, but ice time among forwards is usually less, Bure being an exception with 26:52 for the Panthers in 2000–01. The only other 25-minute men are Jagr who logged 25:51 in 1998–99; Sakic with 25:35 in 1998–99; and Bure, again, with 25:00 in 2001–02.

2.5 **A. During the NHL's 30-game schedule of 1924–25.**
Well before modern-day players Jimmy Carson and Bob Kudelski set a regular-season standard of 86 games, defenseman Lionel Hitchman played 31 games in a 30-game schedule, splitting 1924–25, 12 games with the Ottawa Senators and 19 games with the Boston Bruins. It was the first time an NHLer played more games than the regular-season schedule. Hitchman went on to his greatest years with the Bruins. He was paired on the blueline with Eddie Shore, a puck rusher who fit perfectly with the stay-at-home defenseman.

2.6 **B. Stan Mikita in 1967–68.**
With his Art Ross Trophy win in 2003–04 Martin St. Louis may have single-handedly set hockey back a few decades. His league-high 94 points was the lowest point total since Mikita's 87 in 1967–68, when teams played 74-game schedules. St. Louis's height is another throwback to a bygone era. At five-foot-nine and 183 pounds he ranks as the smallest scoring leader since the five-foot-nine, 169-pound Mikita, if you believe the league and team media guides. Anyone who has stood next to St. Louis might give him at best five-foot-seven, shorter than mighty mites Ted Lindsay and Marcel Dionne, who, at five-foot eight, won the scoring crowns in 1950 and 1980, respectively.

2.7   **C. 124 goals allowed; 90 disallowed.**
Of the 6,530 goals scored in 2002–03, 124 were in dispute until the video goal judge determined the puck had entered the net. Another 90 potential goals were disallowed.

2.8   **A. Nathan Horton of the Florida Panthers.**
After being taken down by Philadelphia's John LeClair, Horton was awarded a penalty shot and, according to Florida coach Rick Dudley, "did what good penalty shot people do." The rookie centre waited until goalie Jeff Hackett made a move and tacked it top shelf. "It happened so fast, I didn't have enough time to think about the shot," said Horton. "If I had more time, I might have been more nervous. I was either going to go high or go to my backhand. The top shelf was there, so I went up and it went in." Horton's goal came at 3:38 of the second period on January 8, 2004. He was 18 years, 224 days old, only 38 days younger than Toronto's Jack Hamilton, who established the record on February 19, 1944.

2.9   **B. Eight days.**
A few NHLers have had penalty shot opportunities in less time than Milan Hedjuk, but no one has capitalized with fewer nights between goals. In 1967–68, Toronto's Mike Walton had penalty shots in successive nights but failed to score on his second attempt. Joe Nieuwendyk got two freebies four days apart in 1988–89 and scored once. Then, rookie Esa Pirnes was thwarted twice on October 12 and 14, 2003. Hedjuk's NHL mark was set five games and eight days apart—January 11 and January 19, 2004—on penalty shot goals against Chicago's Michael Leighton and Nikolai Khabibulin of Tampa Bay. Both goals were scored with wrist shots high on the glove in 5–4 wins by Colorado. The goal against Leighton came in the second period and trimmed the Blackhawks' lead to 3–2. Hedjuk's goal on Khabibulin was more special, a game-winning goal in overtime, only the third overtime game-winner in NHL history. After waiting six years for a penalty shot chance Hedjuk connected on two, little more than a week apart.

2.10 C. Four straight game-winners.

An odd distinction to be sure. Even weirder, it was not until Artem Chubarov's third season that he notched a goal that wasn't a game-winner. The Russian rookie scored once in 49 games with the Canucks in 1999–2000. He played only one game in his second year, then potted three more consecutive game-winners in 2001–02 before the string ended.

2.11 B. In 1962–63 when Gordie Howe was goal leader.

Not since Howe topped the league with 38 goals in 1962–63 has anyone won the title with fewer goals than Jarome Iginla, Rick Nash and Ilya Kovalchuk, who shared the Maurice "Rocket" Richard Trophy in 2003–04 with 41 goals each. Peter Bondra led with 34 goals in 1994–95, the lockout year.

2.12 C. Four defensemen.

As of 2003–04, Phil Housley, Brian Leetch, Chris Chelios and Gary Suter all ranked among the top 10 U.S. scorers. Housley

Top 10 U.S.-born point leaders*

PLAYER	YEARS	GOALS	ASSIST	POINTS
Phil Housley	1982–2004	338	894	1,232
Jeremy Roenick	1988–2004	475	645	1,120
Mike Modano	1989–2004	458	648	1,096
Joe Mullen	1979–1997	501	561	1,063
Pat LaFontaine	1984–1998	468	545	1,013
Brian Leetch	1988–2004	242	745	996
Neal Broten	1980–1997	289	634	923
Chris Chelios	1983–2004	178	736	914
Gary Suter	1985–2002	203	641	844
Keith Tkachuk	1992–2004	431	401	832

*Current to 2003–04

retired in 2003–04 as the most prolific U.S.-born scorer with
1,232 points. Many of his best-scoring years were as a Winnipeg
Jet after his trade for Dale Hawerchuk in 1990. In successive
seasons with the Jets, the fleet-footed rearguard scored 76, 86
and 97 points, the last as a contributor to 56 of Teemu
Selanne's record 76-goal and 132-point rookie season.

2.13   C. A differential of 41.

In Brett Hull's case, it is always better to receive than to give.
No NHLer has a higher goals-to-assist differential than Hull,
who recorded a league-busting 41 on 86 goals and 45 assists in
1990–91. The only other player to score at least 40 more goals
than assists in a season is Joe Malone who notched 44 goals
and four assists in 1917–18. But Malone's numbers are suspect,
considering that proper tabulation for assists only began the
following season, 1918–19.

2.14   C. Bill Cowley of the Boston Bruins.

It might be the most costly gesture of sportsmanship in NHL
play. After a game on January 16, 1943, between the Bruins and
the Rangers, Cowley sent a letter to NHL president Red Dutton,
explaining that he didn't feel he deserved an assist that he had
been credited with during the game. Dutton granted Cowley's
request, and deleted the assist from his record. The Bruins centre finished the season second in the scoring race with 72
points (27 goals and 45 assists), one point behind Chicago's
Doug Bentley. The point that was removed from Cowley's stats
left him one assist shy of his own NHL record and cost him the
bonus the Bruins would have paid him for setting a new
record. The extra point also cost Cowley perfect symmetry in
his career stats. He finished with 548 points, one less than the
number of games he had played—549.

2.15   A. He scored a goal.

Every season has a few heart-warming stories of college players
who suddenly become NHLers overnight after a regular goes

down with an injury. For some, fate turns their dreams into reality, at least for one game. University of British Columbia third-stringer Chris Levesque made headlines on December 10, 2003, when he signed a one-day amateur contract to backup Vancouver's Johan Hedberg after No.1 man Dan Cloutier hurt his groin at morning skate. Because no goalie was available from the AHL affiliate Manitoba Moose, Levesque got the call. It came while he was in the school library studying for a geography exam. During the game Hedberg collided with Pittsburgh's Konstantin Koltsov, which provided a few anxious moments for the UBC goalie. "I tried to play it cool on the bench and not look too stressed out. Luckily he wasn't hurt bad," said Levesque, who was given the Canucks No. 40. Things turned out differently for University of Massachusetts defenseman Thomas Pock, who got to play in the Rangers game on March 23, 2004. Pock's invite came while he was hanging out with classmates at his off-campus apartment in Amherst, N.Y. That night, on a 50-foot wrist shot against Pittsburgh's J.S. Aubin, Pock hit the rookie jackpot and scored a goal in his first game. "When I was driving down with my roommate," Pock told *The Hockey News*, "I was joking and I told him I was going to score a goal in the game. He was laughing," said Pock. "And I was laughing back like 'Yeah, right.' It's overwhelming." Pock played five more games for the Rangers in 2003–04.

2.16   D. Martin St. Louis in 2003–04.
Until he won the league scoring race in 2003–04, most NHL radars pegged St. Louis as a hockey town not a hockey player. Teams overlook most five-foot-nothings and St. Louis was no exception on draft day. Calgary signed him as a free agent, but couldn't find a reason to keep him under contract after two seasons. The unheralded St. Louis came to Tampa Bay in 2000 and *voilà*. In three seasons under Lightning coach John Tortorella's high-octane turbo offense, he blossomed into an

Art Ross scoring champion. During the year he was named NHL Offensive Player of the Month twice, becoming the first player to capture the honour in consecutive months since Wayne Gretzky did it in December and January of the 1986–87 season. In January 2004, St. Louis led all NHL players with 13 goals and 25 points and recorded a plus-13 in 16 games, as Tampa Bay set franchise records with 11 wins and 24 points in a month. In February 2004, St. Louis had a league-high seven goals and 14 assists for 21 points during a 13-game span. The Lightning finished with a 9–1–1–2 record in February. St. Louis had points in 12 of those 13 games, including an 11-game point streak.

2.17 C. A goal, an assist and a fight in a game.
Gordie Howe was every sniper, passer and battler who ever laced up skates. He was both Mr. Hockey *and* Mr. Elbows. On an almost nightly basis he picked his enemies apart, settling scores in the net and the penalty box with every weapon at his disposal, which meant his stick for a goal and an assist, and his elbows or fists for a fight. While leading all scorers with 1,850 points, Howe amassed numbers almost equivalent in the box, 1,685 penalty minutes between 1946–47 and 1979–80.

2.18 B. Four shorthand points.
In a 7–4 win against the Vancouver Canucks on April 7, 1995, Winnipeg Jets forward Keith Tkachuk scored a league-record four shorthand points on two goals and two assists while the Jets were playing a man short. Tkachuk earned two shorthand points from assists on goals by Nelson Emerson and Darrin Shannon while the Canucks Brent Thompson was serving an instigator penalty for fighting with Gino Odjick. He later added shorthand goals when Dave Manson was off for holding and Shannon in the box for hooking.

2.19 **C. Four five-goal games.**
Three seasons—1917–18, 1919–20 and 1981–82—saw individuals record five-goal games on four different occasions. During its formative years the NHL witnessed a few great scorers dominate the league with a disproportionate number of five-goal and six-goal efforts. One or two goalies were usually responsible for all the big scores, including the only seven-goal game by a player. History repeated itself in 1981–82. Philadelphia netminder Pete Peeters was the goat, tying old-timer Howard Lockhart, who allowed three of the record four games that had five-goal scorers that year.

2.20 **C. Sidney Crosby of the Rimouski Oceanic.**
After calling premium prospect Sidney Crosby a "hot dog" for his enthusiastic goal-scoring celebrations, Cherry got lots of ink for riding the 16-year-old kid with the "Next One" label. Perhaps the best observation belonged to Jack Todd of the *Gazette* in Montreal, who wrote: "Are we missing something here? Don Cherry is the guy who made himself rich and famous by dressing like a cross between Liberace and Superfly—and he's calling the kid a hot dog?" After hearing Cherry's comment, Crosby, defying his tender age, coolly said, "When I score a goal, I'm going to be happy." Months later, at the 2004 World Junior Championships, the scoring phenom had occasion to pump it up again after becoming the youngest Canadian to score at the World Juniors in a 7–2 win against Switzerland on December 28, 2003.

2

Lefties & Righties

IN NHL HISTORY only eight goalies manning the pipes with a right-hand catching glove have won the Vezina Trophy. Why do so many goalies catch with their left hand? Netminders feel they have better control of their stick with the more dominant right hand, so they catch left. In this game, match the team and year with the Vezina righties and lefties.

LEFTIES

1. _____ Martin Brodeur	A. Toronto Maple Leafs 1941
2. _____ Glenn Hall	B. Montreal Canadiens 1992
3. _____ Turk Broda	C. Detroit Red Wings 1955
4. _____ Ron Hextall	D. Buffalo Sabres 1999
5. _____ Terry Sawchuk	E. Chicago Blackhawks 1963
6. _____ Dominik Hasek	F. New Jersey Devils 2003
7. _____ Billy Smith	G. Philadelphia Flyers 1987
8. _____ Patrick Roy	H. New York Islanders 1982

RIGHTIES

1. _____ Jose Theodore	A. Chicago Blackhawks 1932
2. _____ Chuck Gardiner	B. New York Rangers 1940
3. _____ Grant Fuhr	C. Montreal Canadiens 1944
4. _____ Bill Durnan	D. Chicago Blackhawks 1970
5. _____ Tom Barrasso	E. New York Rangers 1971
6. _____ Gilles Villemure	F. Buffalo Sabres 1984
7. _____ Dave Kerr	G. Edmonton Oilers 1988
8. _____ Tony Esposito	H. Montreal Canadiens 2002

Solutions are on page 121

3

Three-Ring Circus

THE STORYLINE WAS supposed to be Dominik Hasek rescuing the Red Wings, Curtis Joseph getting traded and Manny Legace riding the pines. Instead Detroit GM Ken Holland got a three-ring goaltending circus that saw Hasek go down with a season-ending groin injury after 14 decisions, Joseph hobbled with an ankle injury that limited him to 29 matches and Legace carrying the bulk of the workload, backstopping a team-high 38 games. Still, Detroit claimed the regular-season with 109 points in 2003–04. How do you spell d-e-e-p?

Answers are on page 40

3.1 **According to Florida Panthers goalie Roberto Luongo, where does a netminder suffer the worst pain?**

A. In the collarbone

B. In the groin

C. In the neck

D. In the catching hand

3.2 **Both Martin Brodeur and Partrick Roy have recorded 400 wins, but how much younger was Brodeur than Roy when he notched his 400th?**

A. 66 days

B. 166 days

C. One year and 166 days

D. Two years and 166 days

3.3 In what year was the first net cam used in an NHL goalie net?

A. 1951
B. 1961
C. 1971
D. 1981

3.4 Which goalie set a modern-day NHL record for the longest shutout sequence during the 2003–04 season?

A. Marty Turco of the Dallas Stars
B. Brian Boucher of the Phoenix Coyotes
C. Martin Brodeur of the New Jersey Devils
D. Jose Theodore of the Montreal Canadiens

3.5 When Brian Boucher set a modern-day mark for longest consecutive scoreless minutes (332:01) in 2003–04, how close did the Phoenix goalie come to breaking the all-time record?

A. Under 10 minutes
B. Between 10 and 60 minutes
C. Between 60 and 120 minutes
D. More than 120 minutes

3.6 Which goalie recorded the most NHL wins after his 39th birthday?

A. Johnny Bower
B. Jacques Plante
C. George Hainsworth
D. Gerry Cheevers

3.7 What is the fewest number of career games played by a goalie who recorded only one shutout?

A. One game
B. Two games
C. Four games
D. Eight games

3.8 What is the fewest number of career games played by a goalie who shut out the opposition in his first NHL game?

A. Three games
B. Six games
C. Nine games
D. 12 games

3.9 After retiring from hockey in 2003, what suggestion did Patrick Roy have to increase goal scoring?

A. Increase the size of the nets
B. Play five men aside
C. Reduce the size of goalie equipment
D. Eliminate the trap

3.10 Which NHL goalie played Team USA goalie Jim Craig in the action scenes of *Miracle,* a new feature-length film about the 1980 U.S. Olympic gold medal win in men's hockey?

A. Jim Craig
B. Tom Barrasso
C. Bill Ranford
D. Chris Osgood

3.11 Which NHL goalie set a modern-day record for the best goals-against average in 2003–04?

A. Montreal's Jose Theodore
B. Dallas's Marty Turco
C. New Jersey's Martin Brodeur
D. Calgary's Miikka Kiprusoff

3.12 What symbol did Pittsburgh rookie Marc-Andre Fleury paint on his mask to represent Canada at the 2004 World Junior Hockey Championships in Helsinki?

A. A red maple leaf
B. A flying puck and stick

C. An igloo and penguins
D. A Canadian one-dollar coin, a.k.a. a lucky loonie

3.13 Which goalie was known as Jimmy Buffer to his teammates in 2003–04?
A. Ed Belfour of the Toronto Maple Leafs
B. Manny Legace of the Detroit Red Wings
C. Nikolai Khabibulin of the Tampa Bay Lightning
D. Martin Brodeur of the New Jersey Devils

3.14 What is the greatest number of shutouts posted by a father-and-son goaltending duo?
A. 12 shutouts
B. 24 shutouts
C. 36 shutouts
D. 48 shutouts

3.15 Which country produced the first Olympic goalie to backstop an NHL team?
A. Canada
B. USA
C. England
D. Sweden

3.16 Which goalie faced the most shots in one season?
A. Curtis Joseph of the St. Louis Blues in 1993–94
B. Felix Potvin of the Toronto Maple Leafs in 1996–97
C. Dominik Hasek of the Buffalo Sabres in 1997–98
D. Roberto Luongo of the Florida Panthers in 2003–04

3.17 What is the greatest number of shutouts recorded by all NHL teams in one season?
A. 152 shutouts
B. 172 shutouts
C. 192 shutouts
D. 212 shutouts

3.18 After Patrick Roy retired in 2003, who did the Colorado goalie say he feared most on a breakaway during his playing days?

A. Jaromir Jagr
B. Pavel Bure
C. Wayne Gretzky
D. No one

Three-Ring Circus

Answers

3.1 **B. In the groin.**

When asked by *The Miami Herald* to rank the worst three pains a goalie feels, Roberto Luongo said the nastiest hurt comes from a hit to the mid-body. "First is the worst, and you know where I'm talking about without even having to tell you. Let's call it the jock-strap area. Second is when you get hit in the neck with a shot. And third is getting hit in the collarbone. That feels like someone takes a baseball bat and swings it right at you as hard as they can. The pain can stay with you for weeks," said Luongo.

3.2 **C. One year and 166 days.**

Based on these numbers, Martin Brodeur could blow by Roy and a few other legends to dominate hockey's most important goaltending records. Roy was 33 years and 123 days old when he registered his 400th win on February 5, 1999; Brodeur was 31 years and 322 days old for win No. 400, a 4–3 overtime victory against the Florida Panthers on March 23, 2004. New Jersey's Scott Niedermayer scored with 1:05 left in the extra period. Brodeur achieved the milestone in fewer games than any other goalie and was 400–215–105 in 12 seasons. "The scary thing about Martin is that there is a lot more left," Devils coach Pat Burns said. "He loves the game and he works hard at it and he's only 31 years old." Brodeur is the eighth and youngest goalie to reach the landmark. He also became the first to win 400 playing every game for the same team. "Not to take anything away from the other guys, but it's tough for an organization to have success for so long," Brodeur said. "It definitely makes it special. It says a lot about the success of the organization."

3.3 B. 1961.

The first net cam shots probably came from the wide-angle Nikons of *Sports Illustrated* photographer John Zimmerman, who mounted two cameras on the goal's back pipe at Madison Square Garden in 1961. After receiving permission from Rangers officials (who couldn't find anything in the NHL rule books prohibiting it), Zimmerman had rink personnel chip though the ice to install remote wires from his cameras to his seat directly behind the net and then resurface the ice.

3.4 B. Brian Boucher of the Phoenix Coyotes.

Boucher is not the first nobody to put his name in the NHL record book, but even among the unlikeliest candidates to break Bill Durnan's 1949 modern-day shutout record of 309:21, his candidacy would be a stretch. Boucher, a backup for most of his five-year career, was riding the pines in Phoenix as the No. 3 man after getting beat out by Zac Bierk as Sean Burke's caddy at camp in 2003–04. It only got worse when the Coyotes put him on waivers and there were no takers. Then, in late December, fate came calling. Injuries opened up a spot and Boucher seized the day. His streak began in Nashville on December 22 in a 3–3 tie against the Predators. After giving up a goal at 19:15 of the second period to Scott Walker, Boucher barred the door with a 4–0 win against Los Angeles on December 31, followed by road victories over Dallas 6–0, Carolina 3–0, Washington 3–0 and Minnesota 2–0. Boucher's run ended with a goal he had no way of stopping. A wrist shot fired by Atlanta's Randy Robitaille glanced off the chest of

Phoenix defenseman David Tanabe and into the net at 6:16 of the first period in a 1–1 tie against the Thrashers on January 11. The Woonsocket, R.I., native broke two 55-year-old records by reeling off five straight shutouts and not allowing a goal for 332 minutes and one second. In that span he made 146 saves but, according to Tanabe, Boucher's real test may have come when he wasn't even practising with the team in November. "A lot of us sat back and watched the professional way he reacted to that... those things earn a lot of respect from team-mates, and it makes you proud to stand in front of the guy and do everything you can," said Tanabe. Boucher, holder of more than five hours of shutout hockey, was humbled by the accomplishment. "There's a lot of history in this game and to be a small part of it is something I'm very proud of," he said.

3.5 D. More than 120 minutes.

Boucher's five straight shutouts from December 31 to January 9, 2003, broke Bill Durnan's modern-day record of four zeroes in 1948–49, but it fell far short of the all-time mark set by Alex Connell of the old Ottawa Senators. Playing in an era before forward passing was allowed, Connell stoned opponents in six games for 461 minutes and 29 seconds, besting Boucher's shutout sequence of 332 minutes and one second by more than two complete games, 129:28.

3.6 C. George Hainsworth.

Despite a lengthy and successful pro career before the NHL came calling, Hainsworth still figured he had something to prove after joining the league in 1926–27. He was old enough to retire at 31 years old, but the future Hall of Famer played ironman for the next 10 complete seasons, uninterrupted except for two games in 1929–30 when Montreal won its first of two back-to-back Cups. In 1934–35's 48-game schedule, Hainsworth won 30 games for Toronto, tops in NHL history among goalies aged 39 or older. But that number could be bettered by another Maple Leaf goalie, Ed Belfour, who turned in a 34-win season at age 38 in 2003–04. One more solid season for Belfour and he would rewrite this record and break Hainsworth's 70-year hold.

Most wins by goalies aged 39 or older*

PLAYER	SEASON	TEAM	WINS	AGE
George Hainsworth	1934–35	Toronto	30	39 yrs., 266 days
Gerry Cheevers	1979–80	Boston	24	39 yrs., 121 days
Jacques Plante	1970–71	Toronto	24	42 yrs., 77 days
Johnny Bower	1963–64	Toronto	24	39 yrs., 135 days
George Hainsworth	1935–36	Toronto	23	40 yrs., 269 days
Tony Esposito	1982–83	Chicago	23	39 yrs., 346 days

*Current to 2003–04/courtesy of The Hockey News

3.7 **B. Two games.**

NHL history is rich in hero-to-zero stories, few more unique than the saga of the two-game career of Joe Ironstone. After allowing three goals in two periods for the New York Americans in a 1925–26 game, Ironstone was sent back to minor pro until March 28, 1928, when he was called up by Toronto GM Conn Smythe to replace an injured John Ross Roach in a Toronto-Boston match. In what proved to be his downfall, Ironstone agreed to play at Smythe's request but not at his price. Because the invite was last-minute on game day, Smythe met Ironstone's demands for a top-dollar wage. The replacement goalie proved worthy of every penny, playing 70 minutes of shutout hockey in the scoreless overtime tie. But Smythe didn't like Ironstone's cheekiness and the goalie never played another NHL game.

3.8 A. Three games.

Dave Gatherum, Gord Henry and Claude Pronovost are among more than 20 goalies who recorded shutouts in their NHL debuts. Unfortunately, the big league wasn't so kind in subsequent games. Each had the NHL lifespan of a fruitfly, backstopping two more games before being swatted back to the minors.

3.9 C. Reduce the size of goalie equipment.

After hanging up the pads, hockey's winningest goalie decided the best way to save the game (and, presumably, his career records) was to shrink goalie gear to help increase scoring. "I'm not going to have a lot of friends with the goalie, but we have to cut their pads back to 10 inches from 12," Roy said at the 2004 NHL All-Star game. Now an owner of the Quebec Remparts, Roy wants more scoring. "I know all my fans went home happy after seeing a 7–7 junior game with my Remparts. I didn't like seeing the seven on my guy, but scoring seven goals? Yeah, I liked that," said Roy.

3.10 C. Bill Ranford.

Ranked by *Sports Illustrated* as the greatest sports moment of the 20th century, Team USA's gold medal win at the 1980 Olympics was nothing short of a miracle. Coach Herb Brooks sold a bunch of college kids on the notion they could do the impossible and beat the unbeatable Soviets. Later, some called it the greatest coaching performance in the history of American sports and the most incredible sales job ever done on the minds of athletes who won "something that just never, ever should've been possible." Broadcaster Al Michaels's "Do you believe in miracles?" phrase best described the staggering upset by the Americans. In the Hollywood blockbuster *Miracle*, producers stocked the cast of the U.S. team with several first-time actors. American goalie Jim Craig was played by actor Eddie Cahill and by Ranford during the action sequences. "To add authenticity to the scenes, I tried duplicating some of Jim's signature moves," Ranford wrote in a story for *The Hockey News.* "I'd try to copy the way he played the puck with his glove hand near the bottom of his stick to help clear it out of the zone, or the way he'd hold his glove high on the crossbar so he could watch guys behind the net," said Ranford. Although it was a 4–2 victory over Finland that officially clinched the gold medal, the real miracle was the previous match, a 4–3 win over the Soviet Union.

3.11   D. Calgary's Miikka Kiprusoff.
He played in less than half of Calgary's games in 2003–04, but Kiprusoff attracted honourable mentions for league MVP after posting a modern-era low 1.69 goals-against average and a striking 24-10-4 record. Along with Jarome Iginla's 41-goal blitz, Kiprusoff's spiffy play led the Flames to their first playoff spot since 1996, a nice career boost considering he was San Jose's odd man out before being plucked in mid-November from the depths of the Sharks system by Calgary coach and general manager Darryl Sutter. Kiprusoff topped Marty Turco's goals-against record of 1.72 in 2002–03 and produced the lowest average by a regular since 1939–40 when Ranger Davey Kerr's 48-game performance netted a 1.54.

3.12   D. A Canadian one-dollar coin, a.k.a. a lucky loonie.
Although it brought gold to Canada's teams three times in international competition, the loonie lost some of its luster at the World Juniors in 2004. Each side of Fleury's mask was decorated with each side of the coin—a loon and a portrait of Queen Elizabeth. But maybe the obvious tempted fate too much. Canada had a 3–1 lead in the third period evaporate on three weird goals by Team USA, including the tournament winner which came when a routine clearing pass by Fleury bounced off teammate Braydon Coburn, flipped back into the Canadian crease and dribbled slowly over the goal line. Fleury belly-flopped into his net, desperate to stop the fluke goal. Despite some big stops, the loonie-laden Fleury was clearly the

team goat. And he knew it. "The first one hit my shoulder and went in the net. The second one hit my stick, bounced over my head, and went in the net. The third one, I chipped off my D and it went in again," said Fleury. Bad luck can't be blamed for blowing a 3–1 lead and losing the gold, but it will be some time before another Canadian goalie sports headgear with a loonie design. Fleury's mask motif was conceived by 18-year-old Tanner Klassen of Campbell River, B.C., who submitted the winning design in a Hockey Canada contest.

3.13   B. Manny Legace of the Detroit Red Wings.
Detroit's backup since 2000–01, Legace kept finding himself in the spotlight during 2003–04. With a us$15-million stable of goalies to contend with, the Red Wings still had trouble handing their No. 1 job to, well, their No. 1 goalies, after an injury epidemic felled both Dominik Hasek and Curtis Joseph. The Wings' No. 3 man, Legace, drew the most assignments in the goaltending soap opera. He became the man in the middle, literally. Because Legace's locker was located in no-man's land between the stalls of Hasek and Joseph, teammates called him Jimmy Buffer, presumably, a reference to singer Jimmy Buffet.

3.14   A. 12 shutouts.
Three pairs of father-and-son combos have each netted a combined total of 12 shutouts, with two pairs—Ron and John Grahame and Bob and Brent Johnson—competing to top that count, since both John Grahame and Brent Johnson were active in 2004–05. Pat and Dennis Riggin were the first father-and-son duet to total 12 zeroes between them.

3.15   B. USA.
Jack McCartan didn't survive long in the NHL after winning the gold medal for the United States in 1960: just eight games with the New York Rangers. But it was long enough to claim this NHL first.

3.16 D. Roberto Luongo of the Florida Panthers in 2003–04.

Never mind being named Florida's most valuable player, Luongo would have been a strong candidate for the Hart Trophy as league MVP had the Panthers reached the playoffs. He was a warrior through 72 games, battling 2,475 shots to establish a new NHL record and break Felix Potvin's old mark of 2,438 in 1996–97. Luongo also set a new league record with 2,303 saves, allowing only 172 goals for a .931 save percentage, third best in the league during 2003–04. He recorded seven shutouts on the 24th place overall Panthers. His most impressive work may have come in the three games in which he faced 50 shots. Luongo won two and was 7-7-5 in games with 40 or more shots. It is hard to imagine how bad Florida would have been without him.

3.17 C. 192 shutouts.

In 2003–04, five teams reached double-digit shutout counts to help produce the highest total of zeroes by all teams in league history: 192. New Jersey led the parade of zilches with 14, followed by Toronto, Calgary and San Jose's 11. Dallas had 10. Lowly Washington and Pittsburgh recorded just three shutouts each. The next best season for whitewashes was in 2000–01 when teams chalked up 186.

3.18 D. No one.

Roy never lacked attitude. It proved as important to his success as any skill or piece of equipment in his arsenal. And he left no doubt when he retired that he feared no player. "I've always had confidence in my abilities—so to be honest, no one." Then Roy, love him or hate him, snickered at his cockiness, adding: "I guess things haven't changed, eh?"

Bench Boss Blues

IN NHL HISTORY ONLY one man has won the Jack Adams Award as coach of the year with the same team he set an NHL record as a player. Unscramble the names of these other Jack Adams winners by placing each letter in the correct order in the correct boxes. To help, each name starts with the bolded letter. Next, unscramble the three letters in the square-shaped boxes to spell out the first name of our secret coach; then all the circled boxes for the family name; and all the diamond-shaped boxes for his team.

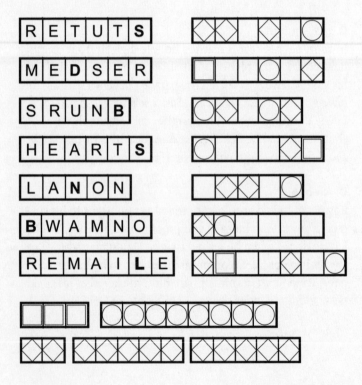

Solutions are on page 121

4

Around the Circuit

SOME OF THE GAME'S most important records are its least recognized because they happen at the league level. For example, the NHL has produced only a handful of 50-goals-in-50-game scorers, but which year yielded the greatest number of 50-in-50 men league wide? Only one season, 1984–85, when Edmonton's Wayne Gretzky and Jari Kurri joined this exclusive club by notching their 50th goals in games No. 49 and No. 50 respectively. Gretzky potted his 50th in the Oilers' 49th game; Kurri missed a few matches due to injury and got his in the club's 53rd game. In this chapter we go around the circuit for a league-wide perspective.

Answers are on page 54

4.1 **What is the greatest number of goals scored by all NHL teams in one season?**
A. Between 4,000 and 5,000 goals
B. Between 5,000 and 6,000 goals
C. Between 6,000 and 7,000 goals
D. More than 7,000 goals

4.2 **What is the greatest number of power-play goals scored by all teams in one season?**
A. 1,481 power-play goals
B. 1,781 power-play goals
C. 2,081 power-play goals
D. 2,381 power-play goals

4.3 **What is the greatest number of power-play advantages recorded by all teams in one season?**

A. 9,282 power-play advantages
B. 11,282 power-play advantages
C. 13,282 power-play advantages
D. 15,282 power-play advantages

4.4 **What is the greatest number of shorthand goals by all teams in one season?**

A. 232 shorthand goals
B. 272 shorthand goals
C. 312 shorthand goals
D. 352 shorthand goals

4.5 **What is the greatest number of penalty shots awarded in one season?**

A. 27 penalty shots
B. 37 penalty shots
C. 47 penalty shots
D. 57 penalty shots

4.6 **What is the greatest number of penalty-shot goals in one season?**

A. 14 penalty-shot goals
B. 18 penalty-shot goals
C. 22 penalty-shot goals
D. 26 penalty-shot goals

4.7 **What is the greatest number of penalty minutes amassed by all teams in one season?**

A. Between 39,000 and 41,000 penalty minutes
B. Between 41,000 and 43,000 penalty minutes
C. Between 43,000 and 45,000 penalty minutes
D. More than 45,000 penalty minutes

4.8 As of 2002–03, what is the greatest number of concussions in one season?

A. 54 concussions
B. 74 concussions
C. 94 concussions
D. 114 concussions

4.9 What is the greatest number of hat tricks by all teams in one season?

A. 109 hat tricks
B. 139 hat tricks
C. 169 hat tricks
D. 199 hat tricks

4.10 What is the greatest number of 50-goal scorers in one season?

A. 10 scorers
B. 12 scorers
C. 14 scorers
D. 16 scorers

4.11 What is the greatest number of 100-point players in one season?

A. 13 players
B. 17 players
C. 21 players
D. 25 players

4.12 What is the greatest number of 500-goal scorers in one season?

A. Three 500-goal scorers
B. Four 500-goal scorers
C. Five 500-goal scorers
D. Six 500-goal scorers

4.13 **What is the greatest number of 1,000-point scorers in one season?**

A. Five 1,000-point players
B. Six 1,000-point players
C. Seven 1,000-point players
D. Eight 1,000-point players

4.14 **What is the greatest number of players who shared the lead in assist totals in one season?**

A. Two players
B. Three players
C. Four players
D. Five players

4.15 **What is the greatest number of players who shared the point-scoring lead in one season?**

A. Two players
B. Three players
C. Four players
D. Five players

4.16 **What is greatest number of 100-point teams in one season?**

A. Three 100-point teams
B. Five 100-point teams
C. Seven 100-point teams
D. Nine 100-point teams

4.17 **What is the greatest number of 300-goal teams in one season?**

A. 14 300-goal teams
B. 16 300-goal teams
C. 18 300-goal teams
D. 20 300-goal teams

4.18 What is the greatest number of regular-season and playoff games played by all teams in one season?

A. 1,120 games
B. 1,220 games
C. 1,320 games
D. 1,420 games

4.19 What is the greatest number of overtime games by all teams in one season?

A. 215 games
B. 255 games
C. 315 games
D. 355 games

4.20 In modern-day NHL play, what is the highest per cent of overtime games that resulted in a winner in one season?

A. 29.8 per cent
B. 39.8 per cent
C. 49.8 per cent
D. 59.8 per cent

4.21 What is the greatest number of postponed games in one season?

A. 30 games
B. 40 games
C. 50 games
D. 60 games

4.22 Since 1951–52, what is the greatest number of games cancelled because of foul weather in one season?

A. Five games
B. Eight games
C. 12 games
D. 15 games

4.23 **What is the greatest number of games cancelled in one season?**

A. 168 games

B. 268 games

C. 368 games

D. 468 games

Answers

4.1 **D. More than 7,000 goals.**

Only twice in league annals have all teams combined to top the 7,000-goal mark. On both occasions the goal-count spike occurred during the league's only 84-game schedules, 1992–93 and 1993–94. Schedule length aside, new franchises to beat up on in Ottawa, Tampa Bay and San Jose spiked goal totals to more than 7,000 goals each season.

Most goals scored by all teams in one season*

SEASON	TEAMS	GP/TEAM	TOTAL GP	TOTAL GOALS
1992–93	24	84	1,008	7,311
1993–94	26	84	1,092	7,081
2000–01	30	82	1,230	6,782
1981–82	21	80	840	6,741

*Current to 2003–04

4.2 **C. 2,081 power-play goals.**

Tampa Bay, Ottawa and San Jose got chewed up pretty good by special teams in 1992–93. These first and second-season teams recorded the lowest percentages in killing penalties.

Combined with the new 84-game schedule, the NHL produced the highest power-play count, the only time that the 2,000-goal mark has been broken in league history. The next-highest mark was in 1993–94 when 1,975 power-play goals were scored.

4.3 B. 11,282 power-play advantages.

Expansion may have tweaked the numbers on power-play goals in 1992-93, but better defensive systems and goalies have done their share to reverse trends since then. In 2000–01 there was an all-time league-high 11,282 advantages but only 1,877 goals, about a 17 per cent success rate. In 1992–93, the rate was 20 per cent when the league recorded 2,081 power-play goals on 10,636 opportunities. The 2002–03 season saw the next highest total of power-play advantages with 10,876.

4.4 C. 312 shorthand goals.

Interestingly, the most victimized clubs to allow a goal with the man advantage were not the new teams in Ottawa and Tampa Bay in 1992–93. Although they did contribute mightily to the NHL's greatest goal count in one season, the Senators (11 goals) and Lightning (12 goals) played safe hockey on the power play, giving up considerably fewer goals than season-leaders New Jersey and Pittsburgh at 19 goals. On the scoring side, the biggest contributor to the record 312 shorthand goals was Quebec, who led all teams with 21 and Pittsburgh, whose free-wheeling style of hockey earned 20 goals, just one more than the 19 shorthanded against them.

4.5 D. 57 penalty shots.

While penalty shot calls have risen, scoring mano-a-mano has trended the opposite way. Players once routinely potted goals on two of every five shots. In 2001–02 they managed just one goal in four attempts, connecting only 11 times on 46 blasts. More shots were stopped, 39 saves, than any other year in league history except 2003–04 when goalies again blocked 39 of the record 57 penalty shots awarded. Shooters scored just 18 times.

4.6   **B. 18 penalty-shot goals.**
Referees not only awarded a record number of penalty shots, 57, in 2003–04, shooters also produced their best totals that year, scoring a league-high 18 times. Interestingly, the goal-impaired Minnesota Wild, among the NHL's lowest scoring teams, surprisingly netted the greatest number of goals on penalty shots awarded, four goals on six attempts to reverse the league-wide trend. While all NHL shooters scored only 31 per cent of the time in 2003–04, Minnesota's blasters doubled that figure with a 66 per cent accuracy.

4.7   **D. More than 45,000 penalty minutes.**
The rise in penalty totals during the early 1990s was caused by several factors, including a whack of new rules, such as checking from behind, crease infringement and goalie interference, diving, instigating a fight and high sticking (redefined as above waist height). Three of the top five all-time penalized teams—Buffalo with 2,713 minutes, Chicago with 2,663 minutes and Calgary with 2,643 minutes—amassed their penalty highs during 1991–92, the first year of the new rules. But expansion (from 22 to 24 to 26 teams) and two 84-game schedules were the reasons behind the two highest penalized seasons, 1992–93 and 1993–94. The 1987–88 season was a blip year: the NHL had a record 15 teams with more than 2,000 penalty minutes.

Most penalty minutes in one season*

SEASONS	PENALTY MINUTES
1992–93	45,650
1993–94	45,559
1987–88	44,380
1991–92	43,781

*Current to 2003–04

4.8   C. 94 concussions.
Understanding the severity of a concussion is as elusive as the
reasons for its dramatic increase among NHL players. Since
reporting of head injuries began in the 1990s, the usual sus-
pects—bigger players, modern equipment and harder
glass—have been targeted, but studies suggest that a
newfound respect for concussions has meant an increased
awareness by players and doctors about its seriousness. This
has meant an increase in concussions reported. In 2002–03,
the NHL's injury analysis panel reported an all-time high 94
concussions, a number expected to be surpassed in 2003–04,
at the time of this writing. A concussion occurs when the
brain smacks against the skull after a collision. Several players'
careers have been cut short, including Pat LaFontaine and
Brett Lindros, because of concussions.

4.9   B. 139 hat tricks.
Remember when hockey was about scoring goals? Even
though 1981–82 ranks fourth highest in scoring (6,741 goals), it
leads all seasons in hat tricks. Wayne Gretzky netted an all-
time high 10 three-or-more goal games that year. The 1980–81
season featured the second-most hat tricks: 133.

4.10   C. 14 scorers.
Now in danger of extinction, the 50-goal scorer was commonplace in the early 1990s. An astounding 14 forwards broke the
barrier in 1992–93, led by Euro snipers Alexander Mogilny and
Teemu Selanne, who both notched 76 goals. Three other players broke 60: Pavel Bure, Luc Robitaille and Mario Lemieux.

4.11   C. 21 players.
Stricter officiating and an influx of talented young Europeans
helped to free offensive creativity in the early 1990s. The high-
water mark was in 1992–93, when 21 NHLers recorded 100
points. The list included such unlikely names as Rick Tocchet,
Craig Janney and Joe Juneau.

4.12 B. Four 500-goal scorers.

Almost 30 years after Maurice Richard registered the NHL's first 500th career goal, the league hit another 500-goal milestone: the first season of multiple players who scored their 500th goal. Mike Bossy and Gilbert Perreault each notched No. 500 in 1985–86. Other seasons have witnessed multiple 500-goal scorers, but 1995–96 had a record four, as Mario Lemieux, Mark Messier, Steve Yzerman and Dale Hawerchuk reached the sniper's gold standard.

4.13 B. Six 1,000-point players.

Celebrating the 1,000-point player became a matter of routine in 1997–98 when a record six players—Adam Oates, Phil Housley, Dale Hunter, Pat LaFontaine, Luc Robitaille and Al MacInnis—scored their millennium marker. Hunter, LaFontaine and Robitaille all notched their 1,000th in January alone, the most in one month in league history.

4.14 B. Three players.

Only twice have three players tied for the NHL assist lead, first in 1917–18 when Cy Denneny, Reg Noble and Harry Cameron each recorded 10 assists; and then in 1965–66 when Stan Mikita, Bobby Rousseau and Jean Béliveau each had 48 assists.

4.15 B. Three players.

Three seasons—1961–62, 1979–80 and 1994–95—produced a three-way tie for the scoring lead. Andy Bathgate and Bobby Hull had league highs of 84 points in 1961–62; Wayne Gretzky and Marcel Dionne tied with 137 points in 1979–80; and Jaromir Jagr and Eric Lindros shared the lead with 70 points in 1994–95. Hull, Dionne and Jagr were crowned champions because they had more goals.

4.16 C. Seven 100-point teams.

Multiple 100-point teams in one season are products of expansion and overtime points. To date, there have been four seasons that produced a record seven century clubs: 1992–93, 1999–2000, 2000–01 and 2002–03. Seven 100-point clubs have become commonplace in the 28- and 30-team NHL, but one year, 1992–93, produced a ratio of almost one in three clubs with 100 points or more in the 24-team league. That season Pittsburgh (and many other teams) beat up on expansion Ottawa and Tampa Bay to equal the greatest gap—95 points— between first and last place teams in league history. (The record was first set in 1975–76 when Montreal and Washington had a 95-point gap.) The top 10 clubs amassed 1,033 team points; or more than 50 per cent of the 2,016 points available. The extra point for an overtime loss is another important consideration. For example, in 1999-2000, the first year teams were awarded one point for an overtime loss, three of the seven 100-point teams would not have hit 100 without those OTL points.

4.17 B. 16 300-goal teams.

The arrival of four WHA teams into the NHL in 1979–80 sparked an offensive surge the likes of which had seldom been seen before. Goals-per-game averages skyrocketed to 8.3 in 1981–82, a modern-day high spurred by a record 16 300-goal teams, including the first +400-goal club in Edmonton.

4.18 C. 1,320 games.

The 30-team NHL played 1,230 regular-season and 90 playoff matches between October 3, 2001, and June 13, 2002. Another 116 pre-season exhibition games were played from September 15 to October 1, rounding out the 10-month hockey season.

4.19 C. 315 games.

Extra periods have steadily increased since the NHL adopted the five-minute sudden-death overtime in 1983–84. The +300-game mark was cracked in 2002–03 as one in four games ended in overtime. The rise comes from a defensive style of play, which coaches have embraced even more since the

1999–2000 ruling awarding a point for an overtime loss. Logic dictates: why risk a loss in regulation time when a loss in overtime guarantees a point? But once in the extra period something else happens: that guaranteed point (along with the four-on-four play) appears to create new offense as teams in 2003–04 played a record 315, winning 145 games compared to 170 ties. Previous to 1999–2000, overtimes ended in ties twice as often as a win.

4.20   C. 49.8 per cent.
If the idea behind four-on-four overtime is to encourage teams to go for broke, then 2002–03 was a successful year. Half of the games that were deadlocked after 60 minutes saw a deciding goal scored in the five-minute overtime. Of the 313 overtime games, teams won 156 times in the extra period compared to 157 ties. As of 2003–04, no team has ever produced more wins than ties in overtime.

4.21   A. 30 games.
Winter weather has postponed the greatest number of games but in 1991–92 the culprit was a 10-day players' strike that forced a record 30 games to be rescheduled between April 12 and 16.

4.22   B. Eight games.
Considering the harsh climate that many eastern teams suffer through each winter, it's surprising this number isn't higher. The 1977–78 season was particularly tough on NHL clubs as eight regular-season games were rescheduled between January 4 and March 26.

4.23   D. 468 games.
The line drawn on the ice between the league and the players' union caused the cancellation of 468 games from October 1, 1994, to January 13, 1995. The 105-day lockout lasted one day longer than the 48-game, 104-day season.

Magnetic Attractions

SOME PLAYERS ARE LIKE magnets to silver. Throughout their careers the Stanley Cup follows them from one team to another drawn by mysterious forces that have turned players as such Mike Keane and Claude Lemieux into triple Cup winners. Other NHLers can't get a sniff of playoff action past the second round. In this game, match the two-time Cup winners on the left and their championship teams on the right.

PART 1

1. _____ Joe Nieuwendyk   A. NY Rangers 1994, Detroit 1998

2. _____ Terry Sawchuk   B. Edmonton 1984, Pittsburgh 1991

3. _____ Mark Messier   C. NY Islanders 1980, Pittsburgh 1991

4. _____ Ted Harris   D. Dallas 1999, New Jersey 2003

5. _____ Joe Kocur   E. Edmonton 1984, NY Rangers 1994

6. _____ Bryan Trottier   F. Detroit 1952, Toronto 1967

7. _____ Paul Coffey   G. Montreal 1965, Philadelphia 1975

PART 2

1. _____ Patrick Roy   A. Toronto 1967, Montreal 1971

2. _____ Brett Hull   B. Montreal 1986, Colorado 1996

3. _____ Dick Duff   C. Montreal 1986, Detroit 2002

4. _____ Larry Murphy   D. Calgary 1989, Pittsburgh 1991

5. _____ Joe Mullen   E. Dallas 1999, Detroit 2002

6. _____ Frank Mahovlich   F. Toronto 1962, Montreal 1965

7. _____ Chris Chelios   G. Pittsburgh 1992, Detroit 1997

Solutions are on page 122

5

Dropping the Buck

FEW **PLAYERS CAN** shoot from the hip—or anywhere else on the ice—as well as Brett Hull. When asked by *The Hockey News* in December 2003 about escalating player salaries, Hull said: "Bob Goodenow (NHLPA president) will kill me, but if we're going to be realistic about things, probably 75 per cent of the league is overpaid." Did the Golden Brett include himself among the overpaid? In this chapter we take stock of the business of hockey.

Answers are on page 66

5.1   **Which NHL star goalie refused half his salary in 2003–04?**
   A.   Martin Brodeur of the New Jersey Devils
   B.   Miikka Kiprusoff of the Calgary Flames
   C.   Patrick Lalime of the Ottawa Senators
   D.   Dominik Hasek of the Detroit Red Wings

5.2   **How much did Wayne Gretzky's Heritage Classic jersey sell for in an auction on e-Bay in December 2003?**
   A.   US$6,000
   B.   US$16,000
   C.   US$26,000
   D.   US$36,000

5.3   **Which player led the NHL in sweater sales in 2003–04?**
   A.   Steve Yzerman
   B.   Mike Modano
   C.   Joe Sakic
   D.   Martin Brodeur

5.4 How much was Vancouver's Todd Bertuzzi fined for sucker-punching Steve Moore of the Colorado Avalanche in March 2004?

A. us$202,000
B. us$302,000
C. us$402,000
D. us$502,000

5.5 How much does it cost to attend a five-day hockey camp with Montreal Canadiens great Guy Lafleur?

A. CDN$2,500
B. CDN$4,500
C. CDN$6,500
D. CDN$8,500

5.6 What bizarre financial scheme have some NHLers invested in?

A. New technologies to replace DVDS
B. Loans to finance cosmetic surgery
C. A pipeline in Central Asia
D. A pyramid scheme called "gifting"

5.7 Who made headlines after losing us$5 million in the stock market in 2003–04?

A. Mike Modano of the Dallas Stars
B. Jaromir Jagr of the New York Rangers
C. Vincent Damphousse of the San Jose Sharks
D. Curtis Joseph of the Detroit Red Wings

5.8 What per cent of players earned less than the 2003–04 average salary of us$1.8 million?

A. 40 per cent
B. 50 per cent
C. 60 per cent
D. 70 per cent

5.9 **How much money did the parents of a 13-year-old girl killed by a hockey puck at an NHL game get in a 2003 court settlement?**
   A. us$600,000
   B. us$1.2 million
   C. us$1.8 million
   D. us$2.4 million

5.10 **Which NHL general manager demanded money back from a player in a contract dispute during 2003–04?**
   A. David Poile of the Nashville Predators
   B. Darryl Sutter of the Calgary Flames
   C. Doug Wilson of the San Jose Sharks
   D. Kevin Lowe of the Edmonton Oilers

5.11 **How much did a private bidder pay in 2003 for Team USA's game-winning puck against the Soviets at the 1980 Olympics?**
   A. Between us$1,000 and us$4,000
   B. Between us$4,000 and us$8,000
   C. Between us$8,000 and us$12,000
   D. More than us$12,000

5.12 **Philadelphia's Jeremy Roenick was fined almost us$100,000 for throwing what object at a referee during a game in 2003–04?**
   A. A stick
   B. A role of tape
   C. A water bottle
   D. A helmet

5.13 **Which team first recorded 400 consecutive home sellouts?**
   A. The Toronto Maple Leafs
   B. The New York Rangers

C. The Colorado Avalanche

D. The Boston Bruins

5.14 Which team averaged the highest attendance per game in one NHL season?

A. The Vancouver Canucks

B. The Montreal Canadiens

C. The Detroit Red Wings

D. The Chicago Blackhawks

5.15 Which NHL owner was fined US$100,000 for scuffling with a disgruntled fan in January 2004?

A. Thomas Hicks of the Dallas Stars

B. Mario Lemieux of the Pittsburgh Penguins

C. Ted Leonsis of the Washington Capitals

D. Ed Snyder of the Philadelphia Flyers

5.16 With which hobby was Bee Hive corn syrup once associated?

A. NHL team pucks

B. Hockey cards

C. Game-worn jerseys

D. Autographed hockey sticks

5.17 Which NHL team offered its fans free playoff tickets in 2003–04?

A. The Toronto Maple Leafs

B. The New York Islanders

C. The Nashville Predators

D. The Vancouver Canucks

5.18 How much bonus money did Ottawa's Jason Spezza receive for reaching the 20-goal plateau in 2003–04?

A. Between US$500,000 and US$1 million

B. Between US$1 million and US$2 million

C. Between US$2 million and US$3 million

D. More than US$3 million

5.19 How much money was involved in Montreal broadcaster
Jean Perron's defamation suit against a book publisher
in 2004?

A. cdn$600

B. cdn$6,000

C. cdn$60,000

D. cdn$600,000

5.20 Which NHL team was the first to lose a player to free
agency rather than pay him his estimated worth via
arbitration?

A. The Philadelphia Flyers

B. The Calgary Flames

C. The Boston Bruins

D. The Ottawa Senators

5.21 How many different sweater looks (third jerseys, etc.) were
worn in the 30-team NHL in 2003–04?

A. 36 sweaters

B. 56 sweaters

C. 76 sweaters

D. 96 sweaters

Dropping the Buck

Answers

5.1 **D. Dominik Hasek of the Detroit Red Wings.**
Hasek's unconventional style between the pipes stopped a lot
of rubber during his career, but the Gumby-like goalie may
have saved his most unusual move for 2003–04 when he for-
feited almost us$3 million of his us$6-million salary after a bad
groin limited him to 14 games. A nice gesture of sportsmanship, but the question is why, considering insurance covered
80 per cent of his contract.

5.2   **C. US$26,000**
Every fan who attended Edmonton's Heritage Classic in November 2003 took home at least one piece of memorabilia: their ticket stub to the NHL's first outdoor game. Then, the auctioning of the big-ticket items began. Gretzky's autographed jersey, one of three worn by the Great One during the geezer freezer, received the highest bid on e-Bay, US$26,000. The sweater was purchased by an unidentified Edmonton man, who also spent US$9,600 on a Mark Messier jersey. "I thought it would be nice to keep them together," he said.

5.3   **A. Steve Yzerman.**
Sales of 38-year-old Steve Yzerman's Detroit Red Wings sweater topped all NHL players during 2003–04's regular season. In second place was Colorado's Peter Forsberg and in third was New Jersey's Martin Brodeur. The average age of the NHL's top 10 selling players was 34.8, far higher than other major sports and not a good sign for the league. All told, the NHL reaped US$1.5 billion in sales of its licensed merchandise, which ranked fifth behind the NFL (US$3.2 billion), NBA (US$3 billion), MLB (US$3 billion) and NASCAR (US$2 billion).

5.4   **D. US$502,000.**
Did the sentence fit the crime? In what was hockey's most sensational story of 2003–04, Todd Bertuzzi sucker-punched Steve Moore from behind and then, coming down on top of him, pile-drived his face into the ice, causing Moore a concussion, facial lacerations and breaks to three cervical vertebrae. Bert's roundhouse right to Moore's head was in retaliation for the Avalanche forward's borderline hit on Marcus Naslund in a February 16 game that left the Canuck captain with a concussion. Bertuzzi paid a steep price for following hockey's so-called "code" of retaliation. The Vancouver star put another player's career in doubt; and was suspended the rest of the regular season and the entire playoffs, worth US$502,000.

5.5 **C. CDN$6,500.**
Wayne Gretzky's fantasy camp in Scottsdale, Arizona, is a little
more pricey (US$9,999), but if your indulgence calls for the
Flying Frenchmen, Lafleur's summer camp at Mont
Tremblant, Quebec, includes five days of hockey with the
Flower, Jean Béliveau and Henri Richard for a mere CDN$6,495,
before taxes.

5.6 **B. Loans to finance cosmetic surgery.**
After getting burned in the stock market, several players,
including Sergei Bezerin, Yanic Perreault and Igor Korolev,
became investors in CreditMedical, a company that loans
money to individuals who want to finance elective cosmetic
surgery procedures such as breast implants, liposuction and
rhinoplasty. Run by entrepreneur Michael Scott Smith, a former junior league hockey player, CreditMedical's loan
portfolio in 2004 grew to US$7 million, a rapid-growth business
which only hung out its shingle in 2001. Interest on a loan is
credit-card high, averaging around 18 or 19 per cent (compared
to banks, which lend at prime plus five per cent, or about
eight per cent). The tummy-tuck-and-face-lift business is
worth about CDN$1.3 billion in Canada alone.

5.7 **A. Mike Modano of the Dallas Stars.**
It was Modano's season to forget. After blowing a reported
US$5 million on an off-ice stock-market gamble, the Dallas star
lost focus and his scoring touch, recording just 44 points in
2003–04. It was his worst regular-season total ever, excluding
1994–95's lockout shortened year.

5.8 **D. 70 per cent.**
Although the NHL has never seen more millionaire hockey
players join its ranks, the vast majority of players in 2003–04
earned less than the average wage of US$1.81 million. Based on
unofficial figures from team payrolls, seven out of 10 NHLers
took home less than US$1.81 million and about 92 per cent

made less than US$5 million. From another perspective, based on a year-long report commissioned by the NHL in 2003, the league lost a collective US$273 million. The Levitt Report on league finances estimates 75 per cent of revenues were spent on player salaries and 19 of 30 teams lost an average of US$18 million. Eleven teams made an average profit of US$6.4 million.

5.9 B. US$1.2 million.
No amount of money ever compensates for the loss of life, but the Columbus Blue Jackets, the NHL and Nationwide Arena agreed to pay Brittanie Cecil's family US$1.2 million after the 13-year-old was struck by a puck at a game in March 2002. Subsequent to the tragedy, every NHL arena installed safety netting around the goal area to prevent any further accidents.

5.10 D. Kevin Lowe of the Edmonton Oilers.
In an NHL first, Lowe called for Mike Comrie to ante up US$2.5 million to complete a trade deal with Anaheim after the disgruntled centre turned down Edmonton's qualifying offer of US$1.13 million. Comrie, who had cashed in on a front-loaded US$12-million contract for two-and-a-half seasons of work with the Oilers, cited "philosophical differences" as his justification for not wanting to join the club. Lowe didn't get the money and Comrie was later dealt to Philadelphia for prospect Jeff Woywitka and a draft pick.

5.11 D. More than US$12,000.
There may be larger inventories of hockey memorabilia outside the Hockey Hall of Fame, but few would compare in historical value to Mark Friedland's collection of hockey sticks, pucks and sweaters. The Aspen, Colorado, businessman owns more than 350 NHL game-worn jerseys, including a 1950 All-Star sweater worn by Maurice Richard that cost him US$40,000. Among Friedland's most famous pucks is US captain Mike

Eruzione's game-winner in the 4–3 victory against the Soviets at Lake Placid during the 1980 Olympics. That piece of vulcanized rubber sent the Americans to the gold-medal game, which they won against Finland. The puck cost Friedland us$13,200.

5.12   C. A water bottle.

Jeremy Roenick, like Brett Hull, is no pussy-footer when venting his anger and frustration on national television. After a January 13, 2004, 6–2 loss to the Buffalo Sabres, Roenick, who had been highsticked in the face without a penalty call to the offender, Rory Fitzpatrick, said in a post-game televised rant: "Look at me... I'm bleeding like a stuck pig... how does he [referee Blaine Angus] not see blood dripping all over my face, all over my jersey. Terrible. Absolutely, absolutely, terrible." But Roenick's words came cheap compared to the cost of firing a water bottle at Angus after the referee's non-call on the play. Launched from the Flyer bench, it skipped across the ice and clipped the official just above the skates. A pretty good throw considering the distance, but the indiscretion earned Roenick a gross misconduct and an unsportsmanlike conduct penalty worth a one-game suspension and us$91,463.41 to the NHL Players' Emergency Assistance Fund. NHL commissioner Gary Bettman admitted that the ref blew the call but said Roenick could have got three games for the bottle toss. That touched off another tirade by Roenick, who later decided to apologize for criticizing the league. Perhaps the best quote at that time came from Roenick's wife, Tracy, who said: "I have to look at you across the dinner table. Will you stop messing up your face?"

5.13   C. The Colorado Avalanche.

The turnstiles never stop turning in Denver. The Avalanche recorded its 400th consecutive sell-out against the Phoenix Coyotes on November 6, 2000. Colorado won 2–1 as goalie Philip Sauve picked up his first NHL victory. Colorado's sellout streak is the longest in NHL history and the longest active streak of all major professional sports. The run dates back to November 1995 and includes 199 sellouts at McNichols Sports Arena and 201 sellouts at the Pepsi Center.

5.14   D. The Chicago Blackhawks.
It was the hype surrounding the opening of Chicago's new United Center that caused the Blackhawks to set this record, rather than any great excitement about the team's on-ice performance or the truncated NHL season, which did not begin until January because of a labour dispute. The Hawks averaged 20,818 fans per game, just 46 fans per game more than the runner-up Montreal Canadiens who attracted 20,772 at the Molson Centre in 1997–98.

5.15   C. Ted Leonsis of the Washington Capitals.
In a bizarre incident following a 4–1 loss to Philadelphia in January 2004, Leonsis attacked Jason Hammer after the 20-year-old fan led a derisive chant and held up a sign that read "Caps Hockey; AOL Stock—See a Pattern?" at the MCI Center. According to witnesses, the Capitals owner and vice-chairman of America Online began choking Hammer and security guards had to intervene. Leonsis later apologized but was suspended for a week and fined US$100,000—a little more salt in the wound for the Capitals who had a US$30-million deficit in 2003–04.

5.16   B. Hockey cards.
For thousands of Canadian youngsters from 1934 to 1967 the best hockey cards came from the St. Lawrence Starch Co. Ltd., makers of Bee Hive corn syrup. Compared to today's high-gloss cards, a Bee Hive black & white might resemble those grainy snapshots from your grandmother's family photo album in the attic. But they were magic to the kids who collected them. With a mailed-in proof of purchase—a collar off a two-pound can earned a single photo and a five-pound can was worth

two—fans received a photo of their favourite star mounted on larger colour mattes on a 4¼ by 6¾-inch card. Bee Hives were produced in three series: 1934 to 1943, 1944 to 1964 and 1964 to 1967. The photo promotion proved a bonanza for Bee Hive, which quadrupled production to become Canada's largest selling corn syrup in the 1930s. At its height, more than 2,500 photos were mailed daily from the St. Lawrence business office in Port Credit, Ontario. Today, an entire set of 601 cards, if it exists, is worth CDN$75,000.

5.17 B. The New York Islanders.

After insulting fans with the worst ticket price gouge in recent memory, a 38 per cent hike on ducats for 2003–04, the Islanders owner Charles Wang did a Savaradian spinarama and offered free tickets for the first two playoff rounds of 2004 to anyone who buys a full season-ticket package for the 2004–05 campaign. While the deal netted almost 1,500 loyal fans by the March 21 deadline, it cost the Islanders about US$650,000 per playoff game. Wang said at the time he didn't need approval from the NHL, joking "They let me lose as much [money] as I want, any way I want."

5.18 D. More than US$3 million.

Spezza triggered a US$3.85 million bonus by achieving three of six clauses in his contract, the final component being a 20-goal season. The 20-year-old centre scored 22 goals and earned US$1.2 million in base salary in 2003–04.

5.19 C. CDN$60,000.

In libel action against the book publisher of *Les Perronismes*, Perron claimed the satirical work ridiculed him and damaged his reputation as an on-air analyst. But Justice Daniele Mayrand, the judge in the CDN$60,000 suit, disagreed, stating Perron "could be subject to wisecracks, satire, good-natured ridicule and may be caricatured without his consent." The slim volume of Perron's butchered phrases includes: "Don't bite the midget that feeds you" and "The Nordiques should go get some rookies with experience."

5.20 C. The Boston Bruins.
The first NHLer to become a free agent through arbitration was Dmitri Khristich, who signed with the Toronto Maple Leafs for us$2.8 million after Boston walked away from an arbitrator's salary award in 1999. Khristich, who had two straight 29-goal seasons with Boston, slumped badly in a Maple Leaf uniform, scoring 15 goals before being shipped to Washington where he retired in 2002. The second player to become a free agent via arbitration was Bryan Berard, another Bruin cast-off. Boston refused the us$2.51 million salary given to Berard after an arbitration hearing in 2003.

5.21 D. 96 sweaters.
You know the merchandising game has gotten out of hand when teams that have existed less than five years, such as the Minnesota Wild and Atlanta Thrashers, decide it's time to debut a third jersey. All told, there were 96 different uniforms worn by NHL teams, including two new All-Star team sweaters, in 2003–04. The Canucks, Oilers, Kings, Rangers and Bruins set a new record by wearing five each. The surge was sparked by the launch of the NHL's Vintage Hockey Program, which introduced home and away retro jerseys to the apparel sweepstakes.

Hockey Crossword 2

ACROSS

1. Ranger _____ Mironov
4. Short for Daniel
6. Man advantage or _____ play
9. Steve Yzerman's team and home ice
10. Buffalo second-string goalie Mika _____
12. Devils sniper Patrik _____
13. D-man _____ Iafrate
14. Carolina-Columbus wing Robert _____
16. Goalie makes a stop
19. Edmonton D-man Eric _____
20. Florida team
22. Toronto 1960s Cup winner Ron _____
23. Goalie Arturs _____
26. Montreal D-man Craig _____
27. Opposite of loss
29. Commercial
30. Threesome
31. 1994 Ranger Cup-winner Jay _____
32. He _____ the gloves

DOWN

1. Vancouver D-man from 1998–99 to 2002–03, Murray _____
2. 2003–04 rookie points leader, Michael _____
3. Thin
4. Montreal winger Pierre _____
5. Ranger centre Petr _____
6. Islander great, captain Denis _____
7. 1980s Red Wing winger Paul _____ (no relation to golfer Tiger Woods)
8. Long-time Ranger-Bruin sniper Jean _____
11. Boston's Bobby _____
13. 2003–04 LA centre Sean _____
14. Calgary's 1st choice in 2001, Chuck _____
15. Panthers Lyle _____
16. Detroit D-man Mathieu _____
17. Team from Ottawa
18. Washington team
21. Capital of Canada
24. Style or _____ of hockey
25. Dallas team
28. Playing surface

Solutions are on page 122

6

True or **False?**

AFTER HIS RECORD-BREAKING streak of five straight shutouts in January 2004, Phoenix goalie Brian Boucher collected only four wins during the rest of the season in 27 games played. True or false? It's true, Boucher fell apart after his much-publicized run of shutouts, going 4–17–6 over the next 27 starts to average almost four goals-against per game. Not the performance Coyote GM Mike Barnett expected after trading Sean Burke in early February to make Boucher Phoenix's No. 1 man. In this chapter we change the pace and challenge you to a series of right-or-wrong questions.

Answers are on page 80

6.1 Calgary's Jarome Iginla is the first black team captain in NHL history. TRUE OR FALSE?

6.2 The last player to score on his brother in an NHL game was Phil Esposito, who scored on his brother Tony in November 1980. TRUE OR FALSE?

6.3 At one time in NHL history, all overtime games resulted in a winner. TRUE OR FALSE?

6.4 The only scoreless penalty-free game in NHL history actually had a goal that was called back. TRUE OR FALSE?

6.5 As of 2003–04, none of the players involved in the Wayne Gretzky trade of August 9, 1988, were still active. TRUE OR FALSE?

6.6 The Toronto Maple Leafs and the Montreal Canadiens have played in the greatest number of games in NHL history. TRUE OR FALSE?

6.7 The California/Oakland Seals have played in more NHL games than any other defunct team in NHL history. TRUE OR FALSE?

6.8 Martin St. Louis, winner of the Art Ross Trophy for top scorer in 2003–04, was never drafted into the NHL. TRUE OR FALSE?

6.9 No NHL coach has ever been credited with a *playoff* tie. TRUE OR FALSE?

6.10 Despite a 6–2–2 record and a 1.29 goals-against average with the Phoenix Coyotes in January 2004, a month when he notched four of his NHL record five consecutive shutouts, Brian Boucher was not named the league's defensive player of the month. TRUE OR FALSE?

6.11 In his first game replacing the retired Patrick Roy as Colorado's new No. 1 goalie, David Aebischer recorded a shutout. TRUE OR FALSE?

6.12 No modern-day NHLer has ever played on two expansion teams in one season. TRUE OR FALSE?

6.13 No modern-day NHLer has ever played for expansion teams in back-to-back seasons. TRUE OR FALSE?

6.14 The Toronto Maple Leafs have allowed more goals than any other team in NHL history. TRUE OR FALSE?

6.15 At 2004's trade deadline, New York Ranger GM Glen Sather traded players to every Canadian team in the league. TRUE OR FALSE?

6.16 Hockey was once played during the Summer Olympics. TRUE OR FALSE?

6.17 Every captain of the Original Six teams in 1966–67 has been inducted into the Hockey Hall of Fame. TRUE OR FALSE?

6.18 The name of coach Jacques Lemaire's boat is *The Trap*. TRUE OR FALSE?

6.19 When Pavol Demitra was awarded a US$6.5-million contract in 2003, it became the highest salary earned in an NHL arbitration case. TRUE OR FALSE?

6.20 American coach Herb Brooks, who led Team USA to the 1980 Olympic gold medal, was the final cut on the U.S. Olympic squad that won the gold medal in 1960. TRUE OR FALSE?

6.21 No pro player has played with more than four different teams—NHL clubs or otherwise—in a season. TRUE OR FALSE?

6.22 No player has ever suited up for more than five different Canadian-based NHL teams in a career. TRUE OR FALSE?

6.23 No player has ever suited up for more than six different American-based NHL teams in a career. TRUE OR FALSE?

6.24 The first time the NHL iced 30 teams, in 2000–01, the league topped the 20-million fan mark. TRUE OR FALSE?

6.25 The term "hat trick" originated in hockey. TRUE OR FALSE?

6.26 In 2003–04 the captains of the Edmonton Oilers and the Calgary Flames each hail from their rival's hometown. TRUE OR FALSE?

6.27 No player has ever scored goals in their first regular-season games more than two seasons in a row. TRUE OR FALSE?

6.28 One of Jarome Iginla's other first names is Elvis. TRUE OR FALSE?

6.29 The first time that three players shared the goal-scoring title in regular-season action was in 2003–04. TRUE OR FALSE?

6.30 No modern-day NHLer has ever played for more than two expansion teams in different years during a career. TRUE OR FALSE?

6.31 Only one modern-day player has played with two teams transferred from other cities in a single season. TRUE OR FALSE?

6.32 More goals were scored by all NHL teams in 2003–04 than 2002–03. TRUE OR FALSE?

6.33 When the Tampa Bay Lightning swept Montreal in the 2004 playoffs, it marked the first time that the Canadiens had lost a series in four straight games in franchise history. TRUE OR FALSE?

6.34 One individual has won the Stanley Cup 11 times before his 10th birthday. TRUE OR FALSE?

Answers

6.1 True.

It was a move everybody supported, including Calgary's outgo-
ing captain Craig Conroy, who made the final decision to let
Iginla be captain in 2003–04. "The reason I did it?" Conroy
said. "I've been here awhile and Jarome's matured. He's such a
great player, a leader, everything. It's time for him to take over
this team."

6.2 False.

As rare a commodity as goals are for Mathieu Biron, none has
been sweeter than his marker on November 24, 2003, when
the Florida defenseman scored the game-winner against his
older brother Martin in a 2–1 victory over the Buffalo Sabres.
Despite their three-year age difference, the siblings never
faced each other in junior or minor hockey. "It's something
that you dream about," said Mathieu Biron in an *Associated
Press* story. "It's something you get excited about. We are
always chatting about that during the off-season. Even when I
spoke with him yesterday about scoring against him, he said,
'You wish.' Tonight he won't be talking about that. That's for
sure." The Biron's brother-on-brother goal was the first since
Phil and Tony Esposito connected, while Phil was with the
New York Rangers and Tony was in goal for the Chicago
Blackhawks, on November 5, 1980.

6.3 True.

In the NHL's first four years, 1917–18 to 1920–21, all games were
played to a conclusion, no matter how long it took.
Considering that the arenas weren't heated, there was an
added incentive to get things wrapped up in regulation. As
you might expect this was not a defensive era.

6.4　True.

Officially, the game report for the Chicago-Toronto tilt on February 20, 1944, shows no goals and no penalties recorded, the only such match in league history. But at 9:16 of the second period Chicago's Fido Purpur slammed one past Paul Bibeault only to have the play nullified when referee Bill Chadwick ruled the shot illegal. Apparently, Purpur scored the goal with his stick above his shoulders. The mild–mannered 0–0 draw was played in one hour and 55 minutes.

6.5　False.

Tears in Edmonton quickly turned into wide grins in Los Angeles after Gretzky became a King in 1988. Los Angeles also got Mike Krushelnyski and Marty McSorley, while the Oilers picked up Jimmy Carson, Martin Gelinas, three first round picks and us$15 million. Five years after the Great One retired in 1999, only two members from that transaction were still active. In 2003–04, Gelinas was playing for the Calgary Flames and Martin Rucinsky, who originally came to Edmonton in 1991 as one of three draft picks in the trade, was a member of the Vancouver Canucks.

6.6　True.

As of 2003–04, Toronto and Montreal—the only original charter NHL teams from 1917–18—have played in 5,564 games. Boston is second with 5,386 games since 1924–25.

6.7　False.

There aren't many league records still held by the Brooklyn/New York Americans. Nevertheless, the club's name and its star-spangled sweaters have a place in hockey lore. The Amerks played in 874 games between 1925–26 and 1941–42; California ranks second with 698 matches from 1967–68 to 1975–76.

6.8 **True.**

At least four inches shorter and 20 pounds lighter than the average NHLer, Martin St. Louis was never drafted by an NHL team because most scouts considered him too small to play in heavy traffic at the NHL level. St. Louis spent four years at the University of Vermont and one season putting up impressive numbers in the minors before getting a sniff from Calgary in 1998. The Flames signed him but he managed only four goals in 69 games. St. Louis was released and became a free agent again, signing with Tampa Bay in 2000. Among all players eligible for draft selection since 1969, St. Louis is the only NHL scoring champion who was never drafted.

6.9 **False.**

Several old-time coaches have recorded playoff ties, all coming during an era when many series were decided by total goals (instead of most wins in a "best-of" format) and games could end in ties. Lester Patrick of the New York Rangers leads all NHL coaches with seven ties in postseason play between 1926 and 1939.

6.10 **True.**

Boucher must have been scratching his noodle after the NHL named Ottawa defenseman Wade Redden defensive player of the month for January 2004. Redden led all Senators in ice time as the team earned a season-best 10–4–2–0 record, but Boucher set two modern-day NHL records with five straight shutouts and a streak of 332 minutes and one second without allowing a goal. All but one of his zeroes came in January 2004.

6.11 **True.**

For three years Aebischer had one of the cushiest backup jobs in the NHL. Then, Patrick Roy retired. How would the Swiss-born goalie perform once out of the long shadow of Roy and in the spotlight as the Avalanche's No. 1? Aebischer had a better save percentage (.924) and goals-against average (2.09) than Roy in his last year, and just three fewer wins (32) than the retired king of the crease. In his first game as No. 1, he stoned Chicago 5–0 on October 5, one of four shutouts that he posted in 2003–04.

6.12 False.

Since 1967, eight NHLers have been traded between expansion teams, the most well-known, Bobby Hull, was dealt by Winnipeg to Hartford in 1979–80. The others are Art Stratton and Wayne Hicks in 1967–68 (Philadelphia and Pittsburgh); Jean-Guy Talbot in 1967–68 (Minnesota and St. Louis); Ernie Hicke and Arnie Brown in 1972–73 (Atlanta and New York Islanders); and Ron Low and Ron Chipperfield in 1979–80 (Edmonton and Quebec).

6.13 False.

Since 1967, nine players have switched expansion clubs in successive years, all between 1991–92 and 2000–01, when nine new teams joined the league. No player was unlucky enough to play on three teams in three straight expansion years, although Andrew Brunette came close with Nashville in 1998–99, Atlanta in 1999–2000 and Minnesota in 2001–02, the Wild's second season.

6.14 True.

Age has its disadvantages. Toronto has given up 17,078 goals between 1917–18 and 2003–04, followed by New York with 16,696 and Chicago with 16,136.

6.15 True.

In 2003–04 no GM in the NHL made more trades than Sather, 11 during the season, most coming during New York's fire sale leading up to the March 9 trade deadline. By the time he finished dismantling the mess he had made of the Rangers,

Sather worked a deal with every Canadian-based club. American teams also benefited but not in proportion to their league representation. Sather's biggest deals included Martin Rucinsky to Vancouver; Greg de Vries to Ottawa; Brian Leetch to Toronto; Alexei Kovalev to Montreal; Chris Simon to Calgary; and Petr Nedved and Jussi Markkanen to his former team, Edmonton. Among U.S. clubs, Washington got Anson Carter; Colorado got Matthew Barnaby; and Philadelphia got Vladimir Malakhov. So ended Sather's grand experiment of an all-finesse team on Broadway. Instead he got a team of aging, overpaid underachievers who failed to live up to their talent or income because they didn't care enough about each other to win.

6.16 True.

In 1920, the Winnipeg Falcons won the Allan Cup to become the amateur champions of Canada, an honour that earned them the right to represent their country when hockey was first admitted as a sport at the Antwerp Summer Olympics. It was the first and only time hockey was played at the Summer Games.

6.17 False.

Five of six captains from the last year of the six-team era have Hall of Fame status. George Armstrong (Toronto), Johnny Buyck (Boston), Pierre Pilote (Chicago), Alex Delvecchio (Detroit) and Jean Béliveau (Montreal) all gained Hall entry. The lone exception was Bob Nevin, captain of the New York Rangers from 1964–65 to 1970–71.

6.18 True.

Lemaire, the often-credited inventor of hockey's dreaded trap system of defense, christened his pleasure yacht *The Trap*. Big sense of humour that Lemaire.

6.19 False.

Pavol Demitra's one-year us$6.5-million deal via arbitration in 2003 was the second-highest since arbitration became part of the salary landscape, second only to the us$7 million Philadelphia's John LeClair received in 2000. LeClair had been seeking us$9 million after a previous contract of us$3.7 million with the Flyers. Demitra earned us$3.9 million while leading St. Louis with 93 points in 2002–03.

6.20 True.

Brooks's own failure as a player unable to make the 1960 gold-medal team pushed him to succeed when he became a coach. When the 1960 squad won gold without him, Brooks and his father were at home in Minnesota. "I guess they cut the right guy," the old man said, devastating the younger Brooks. That moment of humiliation drove Brooks to win three national championships as coach at the University of Minnesota and then, before a stunned hockey world, a gold medal for Team USA at the 1980 Olympics.

6.21 False.

Two players—Dennis O'Brien and Dave McLlwain—hold the record for most NHL teams in one season, but neither are as well-travelled as some players such as Rick Tabaracci, who ping-ponged between with six different pro and international clubs in 1999–2000. It was a fitting end to a career that saw the veteran goalie play for seven different NHL franchises. His 46-game season in 1999–2000 included only three NHL matches between Atlanta and Colorado, but he was everywhere, making stops for Canada's National Team at the 1999 World Championships and three different clubs in the IHL, the Cleveland Lumberjacks, Orlando Solar Bears and Utah Grizzlies.

6.22 True.

Michel Petit and Bobby Dollas got kicked around a lot, each playing with a record five Canadian teams. Petit's league-leading 10-team career included stops in Winnipeg, Quebec, Edmonton, Ottawa and Calgary; Dollas suited up for nine clubs, five in Canada: Vancouver, Quebec, Toronto, Calgary and Edmonton.

6.23 False.

As of 2003–04, several players have donned jerseys for eight American-based teams, including Paul Coffey, Doug Crossman, Stu Grimson and 10-team career men Jean-Jacques Daigneault and Mike Sillinger. Only Crossman and Grimson have suited up exclusively for U.S. teams.

6.24 True.

The 2000–01 season didn't produce the most fans in one year but it was the first time the NHL cracked the 20-million plateau in fan attendance. Thirty arenas saw 20,373,379 fans pass through their turnstiles. The following year, 2001–02, with 1,230 games scheduled, the league peaked at 20,614,613 customers; an average of 16,760 fans per game.

6.25 False.

Although several urban legends exist about Toronto and Montreal haberdashers putting the hat in hat trick, the term originated in cricket when teams would award a new hat to a bowler who took three wickets with three consecutive balls. Hockey borrowed cricket's expression, making it their own with stories about hatters such as Toronto's Sammy Taft who agreed to give Chicago winger Alex Kaleta a free hat if he netted three goals during a game at Maple Leaf Gardens in 1939. Kaleta scored three goals and his free hat from Taft to become part of a hockey myth that endures today.

6.26 True.

There's got to be something in the NHL rule book to stop this kind of thing: Jason Smith, captain of the Oilers, hails from Calgary and Jarome Iginla, captain of the Flames, is an Edmontonian.

6.27 False.

There may be a few snipers who have equaled Florida winger Kristian Huselius's feat of netting a goal in first games in three consecutive seasons, but we would be surprised to find another NHLer who has scored those three goals on the first shots of each season, as our research indicates. In 2001–02, the Swedish rookie potted his first career goal on his first shot on net in Florida's first game, a 5–2 loss to Philadelphia on October 4; then, in 2002–03, he netted his first of the season again on his first shot in his first game, a 4–1 loss to Chicago on October 17; and, in 2003–04, Carolina became the third team to find out Huselius makes his first shot count when potted his first goal on his first blast in the Panthers' season-opener, a 3–1 win against the Hurricanes on October 9. Simply amazing.

6.28 True.

Iginla's full name on his birth certificate is Arthur-Leigh Elvis Adekunle Jarome Jij Junior Iginla. Luckily, Jarome became his first name of choice as few hockey players could get away with Adekunle, Jij or even, Elvis, which Iginla inherited from his father, a Nigerian-born, Canadian-trained lawyer who adopted the King of Rock's first name to integrate better into North American society. "He thought it was like Mike or Mark. He didn't realize who Elvis was," Jarome once said. Iginla was born in Edmonton to Susan Schuchard and Elvis Iginla on Canada Day, 1977.

6.29 False.

Three players have shared the lead for goals twice in NHL history. The first season was 1979–80, when Charlie Simmer, Danny Gare and Blaine Stoughton each scored 56 times. Curiously, that season also saw two players—Marcel Dionne and Wayne Gretzky—tie for the points championship, only the second time that had occurred in league annals. The second time three players shared the goal-scoring crown was in 2003–04 when Jarome Iginla, Rick Nash and Ilya Kovalchuk won the Maurice "Rocket" Richard Trophy with 41 goals each.

6.30 False.

Butch Deadmarsh and Poul Popiel. Not exactly household names but these guys produced NHL careers with three expansion teams, all in different seasons. Deadmarsh joined Buffalo in 1970–71, Atlanta in 1972–73 and Kansas City in 1974–75; Popiel played in Los Angeles in 1967–68, Vancouver in 1970–71 and Edmonton in 1979–80. Two other players—Ron Low and Jean-Guy Talbot—suited up with three expansion clubs but both played with two of their teams in the same year. Talbot was with St. Louis and Minnesota in 1967–68, and later Buffalo in 1970–71. Low played with Washington in 1974–75, and then with Quebec and Edmonton in 1979–80.

6.31 True.

Phil Roberto's ying-yang career generated a Stanley Cup during his rookie year with Montreal in 1971 and this oddity in his final season: playing on two teams born out of failure in Kansas City and California. In 1976, each club moved and set up franchises in Denver and Cleveland. Roberto ended his 385-game NHL career as the only player on two newly transferred clubs, the Rockies and the Barons.

6.32 False.

Despite all the rule tinkering to increase goal production, goal counts were down in 2003–04 from the previous season. In 1,230 games the NHL's 30 teams combined to score 6,318 goals in 2003–04 compared to 6,530 goals in 2002–03, for a 5.14 goals-per-game average against the previous year's 5.31 average.

6.33 False.

Tampa Bay's playoff rout of Montreal in the 2004 playoffs was the first sweep in Lightning history, but it was not the first time it had happened to the Habs. The Canadiens had been bounced in four straight games on three previous occasions: in 1952 by Detroit, in 1992 by Boston and in 1998 by Buffalo. Even so, only four sweeps since 1939, when the best-of-seven format was introduced, is pretty impressive.

6.34 True.

Born on February 29, 1936, Henri Richard celebrates his leap-year birthday once every four Gregorian calendar years. When he won his NHL-record 11th Stanley Cup in 1973 with Montreal, the Canadiens captain was actually just nine years old. Beauty.

Backup to the Greats

SCOTT CLEMMENSEN DOESN'T get much attention. There's no fat contracts, shiny trophies, catchy nicknames or sweet endorsement deals in the job as backup to Martin Brodeur. Heck, a little more playing time would be nice, but for the Devils rookie, 2003–04 was still good: three wins, two shutouts and a warm seat at the end of New Jersey's bench. In this game match these famous Stanley Cup–winning goalies and their backups.

PART 1

1. _____ Dominik Hasek/Detroit 2002   A. David Aebischer

2. _____ Gump Worsley/Montreal 1966   B. Bill Ranford

3. _____ Mike Vernon/Calgary 1989   C. Roman Turek

4. _____ Bernie Parent/Philadelphia 1975   D. Manny Legace

5. _____ Ed Belfour/Dallas 1999   E. Charlie Hodge

6. _____ Gerry Cheevers/Boston 1970   F. Wayne Stephenson

7. _____ Patrick Roy/Colorado 2001   G. Eddie Johnston

PART 2

1. _____ Martin Brodeur/New Jersey 2003   A. Ken Wregget

2. _____ Bill Ranford/Edmonton 1990   B. Roland Melanson

3. _____ Ken Dryden/Montreal 1978   C. Don Simmons

4. _____ Mike Richter/NY Rangers 1994   D. Glenn Healy

5. _____ Johnny Bower/Toronto 1964   E. Corey Schwab

6. _____ Tom Barrasso/Pittsburgh 1992   F. Michel Larocque

7. _____ Billy Smith/NY Islanders 1983   G. Grant Fuhr

Solutions are on page 123

7

Teamwor*k*

WHICH TEAM HAS SCORED the most goals in NHL history? As of
2003–04, the Montreal Canadiens have scored 18,285 regular-
season goals. Boston follows with 17,453 goals and Toronto with 17,193
goals. The Canadiens' lead has gone unchallenged since 1957–58 when
the club ousted Toronto, the reigning champion from 1933–34 to
1956–57. The Canadiens were the first crown holders beginning in
1917–18, when the NHL was formed.

Answers are on page 97

7.1 What is the fastest time one team has scored two goals?
   A. Three seconds
   B. Four seconds
   C. Five seconds
   D. Six seconds

7.2 Which team iced the Mattress Line in 2003–04?
   A. The Tampa Bay Lightning
   B. The Vancouver Canucks
   C. The Dallas Stars
   D. The Ottawa Senators

7.3 What is the longest streak by a team scoring the first goal
   in a game?
   A. 10 games
   B. 14 games
   C. 18 games
   D. 22 games

7.4 Which Olympic hockey team saw its country's leading opera company base a musical on its gold-medal perform- ance?

A. USA, 1980
B. Sweden, 1994
C. The Czech Republic, 1998
D. Canada, 2002

7.5 Even though he was not eligible, which NHL team tried to draft 17-year-old Russian phenom Alexander Ovechkin at the 2003 NHL Entry Draft?

A. The Buffalo Sabres
B. The Florida Panthers
C. The Los Angeles Kings
D. The Calgary Flames

7.6 How many points could an NHL team record if they lost all 82 games in a season, in overtime?

A. 22 points
B. 41 points
C. 62 points
D. 82 points

7.7 What is greatest number of points recorded for overtime losses by a team in the five-year span between 1999–2000 and 2003–04?

A. 26 points
B. 30 points
C. 34 points
D. 38 points

7.8 What is the greatest number of regular-season and playoff games by a team in one season?

A. 106 games
B. 108 games

C. 110 games

D. 112 games

7.9 **What is the greatest number of games into a season before two teams combined to score 10 goals in a game?**

A. 19 games

B. 39 games

C. 59 games

D. 79 games

7.10 **What is the greatest number of penalty minutes recorded by two teams in one NHL game?**

A. 319 penalty minutes

B. 359 penalty minutes

C. 419 penalty minutes

D. 459 penalty minutes

7.11 **Which team has gone the longest time without an NHL scoring champion?**

A. The Montreal Canadiens

B. The Boston Bruins

C. The Chicago Blackhawks

D. The Toronto Maple Leafs

7.12 **Which defunct NHL club first used a ferocious-looking animal on its team crest?**

A. The Hamilton Tigers

B. The St. Louis Eagles

C. The Montreal Wanderers

D. The New York Americans

7.13 In what season did the famous spoked B crest on Boston's uniform first make its appearance?

A. 1928–29

B. 1938–39

C. 1948–49

D. 1958–59

7.14 What is the greatest number of consecutive overtime games played in regular-season play by an NHL team?

A. Four overtime games

B. Five overtime games

C. Six overtime games

D. Seven overtime games

7.15 What is the NHL record for most overtime appearances by a team in one season?

A. 25 overtimes

B. 30 overtimes

C. 35 overtimes

D. 40 overtimes

7.16 What is the fewest goals allowed by a team in a minimum 80-game NHL schedule?

A. 154 goals

B. 164 goals

C. 174 goals

D. 184 goals

7.17 Which NHL general manager told fans to stay away if they were going boo his players in 2003–04?

A. Bobby Clarke of the Philadelphia Flyers

B. Glen Sather of the New York Rangers

C. Larry Pleau of the St. Louis Blues

D. Bob Gainey of the Montreal Canadiens

7.18 **As of 2003–04, which team has the greatest number of wins in NHL history?**
A. The Montreal Canadiens
B. The Boston Bruins
C. The Toronto Maple Leafs
D. The Detroit Red Wings

7.19 **Of all defunct NHL teams, which one recorded the greatest number of wins?**
A. The Montreal Maroons
B. The old Ottawa Senators
C. The California/Oakland Seals
D. The New York/Brooklyn Americans

7.20 **As of 2003–04, which team has recorded the greatest number of losses in NHL history?**
A. The Toronto Maple Leafs
B. The Chicago Blackhawks
C. The Detroit Red Wings
D. The New York Rangers

7.21 **Of all defunct NHL teams, which one recorded the greatest number of losses?**
A. The California/Oakland Seals
B. The New York/Brooklyn Americans
C. The old Ottawa Senators
D. The Montreal Maroons

7.22 **Which team iced the so-called 700-Pound Line in 2003–04?**
A. The Dallas Stars
B. The Boston Bruins
C. The St. Louis Blues
D. The Philadelphia Flyers

7.23 Who was the first NHL Hall of Famer to have his number retired by a team?

A. Eddie Shore of the Boston Bruins

B. Dit Clapper of the Detroit Red Wings

C. Georges Vezina of the Montreal Canadiens

D. Ace Bailey of the Toronto Maple Leafs

7.24 Which team in 2003–04 recorded the most ties since five-minute sudden-death overtime was adopted in 1983–84?

A. The Boston Bruins

B. The Minnesota Wild

C. The New Jersey Devils

D. The Phoenix Coyotes

7.25 What is the greatest number of goals scored by a team in the biggest third-period comeback in NHL history?

A. Three goals

B. Four goals

C. Five goals

D. Six goals

7.26 Which NHL team hosted a Santa Claus promotion that sparked a wild on-ice melee between periods of a December 2003 game?

A. The Los Angeles Kings

B. The New York Islanders

C. The Boston Bruins

D. The Philadelphia Flyers

7.27 Which NHL team saw three of its players become Canadian Members of Parliament?

A. The Calgary Flames

B. The Toronto Maple Leafs

C. The Ottawa Senators

D. The old Montreal Maroons

7.28 What is the NHL record for the most man-games lost to injury by one team in a season?

A. 329 man-games lost

B. 429 man-games lost

C. 529 man-games lost

D. 629 man-games lost

Answers

7.1   **A. Three seconds.**

Vegas odds-makers wouldn't have given the Minnesota Wild better than a million-to-one odds to crack this 73-year-old scoring record, an achievement that has held since the days of the Montreal Maroons in the 10-team NHL. Since then, four other clubs have equaled the Maroons' mark of four seconds for the fastest two goals. But the unlikely Wild managed goals just three seconds apart after potting third period markers from Jim Dowd at 19:44 and then, with an empty Chicago net, Richard Park at 19:47 to lift Minnesota to the 4–2 win over the Blackhawks on January 21, 2004.

7.2   **B. The Vancouver Canucks.**

After three years of trying to find someone who would make a second line out of Daniel and Henrik Sedin, the Canucks thought they had their sniper for the Swedish twins' puck-control game in right wing Jason King, a Newfoundland native and draft-day gamble picked 212th overall in 2001. In early 2003–04 he led all Canucks with 10 goals and all NHL rookies with 14 points. Things soon cooled off for the rookie (and his line fit for a king), but not before every hockey fan in the Lower Mainland of British Columbia was telling this Newfie joke: "How many Newfies does it take to get the Sedin twins to live up to their potential?" The answer? "One... Jason King." The trio was dubbed the Mattress Line—two twins and a King.

7.3 **C. 18 games.**
During their dynasty years of the 1950s the Montreal Canadiens were the greatest thing since, well, artificial ice was invented. Hockey's most-storied franchise produced some near-unbeatable team records, including this jewel: most consecutive games scoring the first goal. Between October 18 and November 29, 1959, the Canadiens scored the first goal in a record straight 18 games, winning 15 and tying three. The record for a club from the start of a season belongs to Philadelphia and Vancouver. Each team had the first goal in 12 consecutive matches.

Most consecutive games scoring first goal

GAMES	TEAM	RECORD	STREAK
18	Montreal	15–0–3	Oct. 18–Nov. 29, 1959
15	Chicago	10–1–4	Dec. 10, 1967–Jan. 13, 1968
15	Montreal	13–1–1	Feb. 19–Mar. 18, 1972

Most consecutive games scoring first goal from start of season

GAMES	TEAM	RECORD	STREAK
12	Philadelphia	10–2–0	Oct. 10–Nov. 6, 1985
12	Vancouver	8–2–2	Oct. 9–Nov. 3, 2003

7.4   C. The Czech Republic, 1998.

Czech fans in Prague are as fanatical about their hockey as any rabid North American puckhead. They've even taken to the 2004 production of Nagano, the Czech opera company's musical based on that country's 1998 Olympic win in Japan. Performers act out the roles of stars such as Dominik Hasek, Robert Reichel and Jaromir Jagr in the opera about the Czech's passion for the game. One memorable scene includes fans running through the streets chanting "Hasek is god!"

7.5   B. The Florida Panthers.

In an effort to secure the surefire No. 1 pick of 2004 a full year ahead of any other team, Florida chucked the Gregorian calendar and tried drafting Russian sensation Alexander Ovechkin at the 2003 Entry Draft. At the time, Overchkin was 17 years old and ineligible until his 18th birthday on September 17, two days too late for the 2003 draft. But the Panthers choose him anyway, trying to fine-tune the space-time continuum with this theory: since there were four leap years since Overchkin's birth in 1985, there would be four "extra" days, making him old enough to be drafted. In a *National Post* story Professor Norman Murray of the Canadian Institute for Theoretical Astrophysics called Florida's argument "clever." "The usual definition [of age] is not how many days old you are, but how many birthdays you have. Yes, 365 days times 18, that's how many days old he would be on September 11—four days before the September 15 draft eligibility date, but that's not 18 years because years... are actually 365-and-a-quarter days long," said Murray. In reality, birthdays are celebrated by years, not by days, which was how the NHL saw it, rejecting Florida innovative approach to ageing. Instead the team picked Nanaimo Clippers forward Tanner Glass, 265th overall in the ninth round.

7.6   D. 82 points.
Considering today's rules that guarantee a point in an overtime loss, a club could conceivably lose every game of the season in overtime and still earn 82 points, which was once considered .500 hockey and enough to secure a playoff spot.

7.7   C. 34 points.
The Florida Panthers and the Boston Bruins have made the most of the 1999–2000 NHL rule that awarded points for overtime losses. As of 2003–04, each team has lost 34 times in overtime. That's 34 team points for *losing* a game. Hard to understand.

7.8   B. 108 games.
Both the Los Angeles Kings of 1992–93 and the Vancouver Canucks of 1993–94 shared a similar fate during the NHL's only 84-game schedules. Each team eventually were defeated in the Cup finals after playing 24 playoff games.

7.9   D. 79 games.
With scoring in sharp decline, snipers today get fewer blowouts to pad their stats. Teams suffer the same consequence. Here's a half-century old stat that no one bothered to check until St. Louis defeated Edmonton 6–4 on October 21, 2003. The last time two teams took almost as long to score 10 goals was in 1953–54, when there were only 210 games in the entire schedule. That year, the first 10-goal game took place on November 29, 1953, when Detroit thumped Chicago 9–4.

7.10   C. 419 penalty minutes.
It must have brought tears to Dave Schultz's eyes, the way the Philadelphia Flyers pounded it out with the Ottawa Senators on March 5, 2004. Imagine how the Hammer beamed with pride at his former team's 5–3 win in a game that featured five

consecutive brawls in the final two minutes, 16 player ejections and set a new NHL record with 419 penalty minutes (breaking the mark of 406 minutes set in a Boston-Minnesota game on February 26, 1981). Schultz couldn't have been more giddy after learning that his born-again Broad Street Bullies established the highest box time total ever for a team in one game, 213 minutes (surpassing Minnesota's 211); and that the Flyers smashed the league's penalty-minute count in one period, 209 minutes, while their adversaries gave as good as they got, 206 minutes all told for Ottawa. Even Schultz's old teammate, Flyer GM Bobby Clarke, couldn't resist a little revenge, having to be restrained by arena personnel in his search for Senators coach Jacques Martin, who Clarke called "that gutless puke" because of a recent February 26 match which included some high-stick work by Ottawa forward Martin Havlat on Mark Recchi. In all, 20 players got fighting penalties and only five players were left on the bench at the final buzzer. Officials needed 90 minutes after the game to figure everything out. Yes, Schultzie would be proud.

7.11   D. The Toronto Maple Leafs.
As hockey-savvy as Maple Leaf fans are, few would know the name Gord Drillon. That's because most Leaf fans weren't even born when Drillon led the league with 52 points and won the scoring title in 1937–38. New York hasn't seen a Ranger win the crown in almost as long. Bryan Hextall Sr. netted a league-high 56 points in 1941–42.

7.12   A. The Hamilton Tigers.
Long before it became cool to ice teams with names and logos of vicious animals such as the Predators, Sharks and Panthers, the Hamilton Tigers sported a jersey in 1920–21 with gold vertical stripes on a black base and the head of a fierce-looking tiger with long razor-like fangs.

7.13 C. 1948–49.

Unlike Toronto's maple leaf or Detroit's winged wheel, Boston's spoked B wasn't featured on the Bruins uniforms for a quarter of a century. The crest was originally a bear and later a simple B. The spoked B was adopted in 1948–49 to commemorate the team's 25th anniversary.

7.14 D. Seven overtime games.

The 2003–04 Edmonton Oilers squandered leads, suffered through goal-scoring slumps and had trouble stealing a win, but what kept them in their frantic race for a playoff berth (which they missed by three points) was a record-setting seven-game overtime streak in late-February and March. The Oilers went 2–0–2–3, which began February 29 in a 5–4 loss to Dallas. From there, they beat Phoenix 5–4 (March 2), tied St. Louis 1–1 (March 4), edged Chicago 4–3 (March 7), equaled Calgary 1–1 (March 9) and ended the run with OT losses to Colorado 3–2 (March 10) and Vancouver 4–3 (March 12). "It's frustrating," said Shawn Horcoff after the Oilers' seventh overtime game. "We needed two points and these one-point games aren't doing it for us. Time is running out and we've got to start winning hockey games." The previous NHL record for consecutive overtime games was five, accomplished eight times by seven teams.

7.15 B. 30 overtimes.

What started out as an overtime rule to decrease ties in 1983–84 has grown into a kind of game strategy to increase point production, especially after the rule changes of 1999–2000, which brought four-on-four hockey and a point for an OT loss. In 1983–84, only 16.6 per cent of games had an extra period. That number steadily increased to 25.6 per cent by 2003–04 as 315 games ended in overtime. The Boston Bruins set a new record that year with 30 overtimes, followed by

Phoenix with 29 and Colorado with 28. The previous high was 28 overtimes by the Avalanche in 2002–03.

7.16   B. 164 goals.

They've been criticized for being mind-numbingly dull and a negative influence on the game, but the New Jersey Devils are also one of hockey's best defensive clubs ever. In 2003–04, even without injured captain Scott Stevens, the Devils allowed just 164 goals, beating the previous minimum 80-game record of 165 goals set by the St. Louis Blues in 1999–2000. At the 50-game mark New Jersey had allowed only 94 goals, the lowest goal-against count through 50 games since the 1955–56 Montreal Canadiens gave up 91 goals; and just back of the 1953–54 Toronto Maple Leafs and their record low 84 goals. The best modern-day record for a full season belongs to those two teams: both the 1953–54 Maple Leafs and 1955–56 Canadiens allowed just 131 goals in their 70-game schedules.

7.17   D. Bob Gainey of the Montreal Canadiens.

Few sports fans have ever been publicly skewered the way Gainey admonished Montreal fans after they booed their favourite target, Patrice Brisebois, in a November 2003 game at the Bell Centre. Gainey coolly fired back at the boo-birds: "A bunch of gutless bastards, to be honest. They're jealous people, yellow people," he said. "Our message to them is to stay away. We don't need you." That kind of public criticism wouldn't work for just anyone, but Gainey, one of hockey's most respected players and team builders, got everyone on side, including his players.

7.18   A. The Montreal Canadiens.

Little surprise here. Montreal owns first place with 2,849 wins, followed by Boston's 2,564 victories and Toronto's 2,418 wins. Montreal has relinquished the wins record only once since

1917–18, for a 16-year period from 1939–40 to 1954–55 to Toronto. It has held the mark ever since, with Boston taking over second place in the category.

7.19 **A. The Montreal Maroons.**
It's ironic that the first tenants of the old Montreal Forum, the Maroons, are still waiting to hang their championship banners for two Stanley Cups. The all-but-forgotten Maroons won 271 games between 1924–25 and 1937–38; the Senators earned 258 victories from 1917–18 to 1933–34.

7.20 **A. The Toronto Maple Leafs.**
Chicago's current slide into mediocrity has moved the Blackhawks to within sight of the Maple Leafs. As of 2003–04, Toronto has amassed 2,327 losses compared to Chicago's 2,308. Like all franchises, these two teams have had their dark days. Their high numbers mean they've been around longer than most NHL clubs.

7.21 **B. The New York/Brooklyn Americans.**
The Seals quit the NHL just in time. Between 1967–68 and 1975–76, California collected 401 losses, one less than the Americans' 402.

7.22 **B. The Boston Bruins.**
One of the NHL's most dominant lines of 2003–04, the Bruins' 700-Pound Line of Mike Knuble (six-foot-three and 225 pounds), Joe Thornton (six-foot-four and 220 pounds) and Glen Murray (six-foot-three and 225 pounds) combined to weigh 670 pounds. In full gear, Knuble, Thornton and Murray tipped the scales at more than 750 pounds, about half the weight of a compact car.

7.23   D. Ace Bailey of the Toronto Maple Leafs.
On December 12, 1933, Bailey fractured his skull on the ice at
Boston Garden after being belted from behind by Eddie Shore.
The initial prognosis was grim and Bailey's family began planning his funeral, but surgeons managed to repair the terrible
damage in two delicate operations. Bailey recovered, but his
career was done. His No. 6 was retired by the Toronto Maple
Leafs on February 14, 1934. It was the first number retired in
any North American sport.

7.24   B. The Minnesota Wild.
After their first overtime win of 2003–04, which only came in
their 79th match of the 82-game schedule, Minnesota's top
scorer, Alexandre Daigle, summed up the season's lost
chances: "Overtime is probably the reason we're not in the
playoffs," said Daigle. And he may be right. What helped get
his team 83 points—that suffocating defensive style of play—
hurt the club in its 24 regular-season overtimes. Minnesota
won once, lost three times and tied 20 games, a league-high
since five-minute overtime was instituted in 1983–84. Had the
Wild opened up and won (instead of tied) half of those 20
overtimes, the extra points would have given the club more
than the eight points needed for the final playoff spot in the
Western Conference. It's a tough lesson, but proves the adage:
live by the sword, die by the sword.

7.25   C. Five goals.
Toronto's Maple Leaf Gardens was the site of two fatal cave-ins
13 years apart. In 1987, the Flames erased a 5–0 deficit with five
third-period goals, then won the game on a goal by Colin
Patterson at 1:30 of overtime. Alan Bester was Toronto's goalie.
Total elapsed time was 15:28. The Blues' 2000 comeback began
after coach Joel Quennville pulled goalie Roman Turek early in
the third and put in backup Brent Johnson. St. Louis roared

back with six straight goals against Curtis Joseph in 15 minutes and seven seconds, the winning marker coming off the stick of Jochim Hecht, just 18 seconds into overtime. Besides the Leafs as victims, the other constant in the two games was defenseman Al MacInnis, who played for the comeback team in both cases.

7.26   B. The New York Islanders.

It wasn't the kind of publicity the Islanders envisioned for a promotion that offered a free ticket to anyone fully dressed as Santa Claus, but the footage was good enough to lead ESPN's SportsCenter broadcast. There they were, some 500 fans dressed as Santa Claus in a Santa Claus parade on the ice between periods of an Islanders-Philadelphia game at Nassau Coliseum. In a holiday mood, some of the Santas started sliding across the ice. Then, a few ripped off their red costumes to reveal the Islanders rival's sweater, the Rangers' blueshirt. Islander Santas began swarming Ranger Santas, and one Father Christmas was seen yanking at a rival's Pavel Bure jersey. Another Santa carried an anti-Mike Milbury sign that read: "All I want for Christmas is a new GM." Bad publicity aside, no one was hurt and things quieted down in time for the second period to begin.

7.27   B. The Toronto Maple Leafs.

Playing for a team with a maple leaf on the jersey must bring out the patriotism in a player. Three of four NHLers who ran for political office and won a seat in Canada's House of Commons were true blue and white Maple Leafs: Howie Meeker, Bucko McDonald and Red Kelly. The fourth hockey-playing MP, Lionel Conacher, never wore a Leaf jersey. In May 2004, the Maple Leaf–Parliament connection continued when former Toronto GM Ken Dryden announced his intention to run in Canada's 2004 general election. Curiously, another long–time Leaf, Frank Mahovlich, is a Canadian Senator, a political appointment made by the Prime Minister.

7.28   D. 629 man-games lost.

No team has ever been as badly hurt in every skating position, both up-front and on the blueline, as Los Angeles in 2003–04. Injuries cost the club an NHL-record 629 man-games. Concussions sidelined Jason Allison and Adam Deadmarsh, two of the Kings' best scorers, for the entire year (that's 164 games, right there). Then, Ziggy Palffy blew out his shoulder mid-season, Aaron Miller suffered a pinched nerve in his neck after plowing face first into the boards, Lubomir Visnovsky had a freak-fall into the boards and was carried off on a stretcher and Martin Straka got hit on two different occasions—the prognosis: two menisci tears in the cartilage of his knee. The Injury Reserve list also saw Ian Laperrière for a spell. The enigmatic Roman Cechmanek might as well have been in the witness protection program for the number of nights he failed to show up to backstop the Kings. Thankfully, the league's most injury-riddled team had Peter Demers, their trainer for 32 years and more than 2,500 games—probably another NHL record.

Stanley Cup Captains

IN PLAYOFF HISTORY only one team has ever won the Stanley Cup while scoring fewer goals than any other club during the regular season. More impressive, our mysterious team has done it twice, including once with the only goalie to captain a Cup winner. There are 29 names of Cup-winning captains listed below. Their names, such as Wayne **GRETZKY,** appear in the puzzle horizontally, vertically, diagonally or backwards. After you've circled all 29 names, read the remaining 12 letters in descending order to spell our unknown goalie captain.

Scott **STEVENS**

Ted **LINDSAY**

Guy **CARBONNEAU**

Wayne **GRETZKY**

Hap **DAY**

Mario **MANTHA**

Yvan **COURNOYER**

Joe **SAKIC**

Lionel **HITCHMAN**

Cooney **WEILAND**

Kevin **HATCHER**

Doug **YOUNG**

Dit **CLAPPER**

Bobby **CLARKE**

Toe **BLAKE**

Sid **ABEL**

Steve **YZERMAN**

Lanny **MCDONALD**

Syl **APPS**

George **ARMSTRONG**

Jean **BÉLIVEAU**

Denis **POTVIN**

Eddie **GERARD**

Mark **MESSIER**

Bob **GAINEY**

Maurice **RICHARD**

Ted **KENNEDY**

Sprague **CLEGHORN**

Mario **LEMIEUX**

S	H	U	P	U	A	E	V	I	L	E	B
C	T	A	O	H	Y	A	S	D	N	I	L
G	R	E	T	Z	K	Y	R	E	M	U	Y
E	E	N	V	C	L	A	R	K	E	C	O
R	P	N	I	E	H	K	L	A	S	D	U
A	P	O	N	C	N	E	G	L	S	A	N
R	A	B	I	A	B	S	R	B	I	Y	G
D	L	R	G	A	I	N	E	Y	E	Z	N
Y	C	A	H	T	N	A	M	R	R	E	R
D	L	C	O	U	R	N	O	Y	E	R	O
E	K	D	D	L	A	N	O	D	C	M	H
N	A	G	N	O	R	T	S	M	R	A	G
N	S	I	H	I	T	C	H	M	A	N	E
E	S	P	P	A	X	U	E	I	M	E	L
K	N	E	D	N	A	L	E	I	W	R	C

Solutions are on page 123

109

8

Stanley Cup Fever

IT GOES ON IN EVERY NHL city when the playoffs begin. Cup fever. Fans spill out of bars onto downtown streets to join victory crowds; others wear team jerseys to the office; and cars get plastered with club logos and flags. Then, when it's down to the final four, really strange things happen. Newborn babies get named after their parents' playoff heroes. In Calgary, one puckhead got so wound up during the 2004 postseason he painted his new garage with a giant flaming "C." It's playoff mania time.

Answers are on page 114

8.1 **What is the longest stretch between Stanley Cup wins by a player?**
   A. 11 years
   B. 13 years
   C. 15 years
   D. 17 years

8.2 **Which team made history by coming back from 3–1 series deficits twice in the same year?**
   A. The Anaheim Mighty Ducks
   B. The Detroit Red Wings
   C. The Minnesota Wild
   D. The New York Islanders

8.3 **Which Dallas Star was surprised to discover his 1999 Stanley Cup ring being sold on e-Bay in July 2003?**
   A. Guy Carbonneau
   B. Brett Hull

C. Mike Modano

D. Ed Belfour

8.4 **Who was the first individual to have his name on the Stanley Cup as a player, coach and general manager?**

A. Toe Blake

B. Jack Adams

C. Al Arbour

D. Jacques Lemaire

8.5 **How many formal challenges has the NHL received from non-NHL teams to play for the Cup since 1926?**

A. Three challenges

B. Six challenges

C. Nine challenges

D. 12 challenges

8.6 **Who was the only captain to score two Stanley Cup-winning goals in NHL history?**

A. Bill Cook of the New York Rangers

B. Toe Blake of the Montreal Canadiens

C. Jean Béliveau of the Montreal Canadiens

D. Mark Messier of the New York Rangers

8.7 **When was the last time a team won consecutive Stanley Cups with different captains?**

A. During the Toronto Maple Leafs' dynasty years of the 1940s

B. During the Montreal Canadiens' dynasty years of the 1950s

C. During the Edmonton Oilers' dynasty years of the 1980s

D. It has never happened

8.8 **Which player matched Maurice Richard's playoff record for career overtime goals during the 2004 postseason?**

A. Peter Forsberg of the Colorado Avalanche

B. Steve Yzerman of the Detroit Red Wings

C. Vincent Damphousse of the San Jose Sharks

D. Joe Sakic of the Colorado Avalanche

8.9 What is the greatest number of Canadian teams to qualify for the playoffs in one year?

A. Four teams
B. Five teams
C. Six teams
D. Seven teams

8.10 Which team's surprising collapse during the 1930 Stanley Cup playoffs is credited with bringing about the best-of-five format in the finals?

A. The Montreal Canadiens
B. The Boston Bruins
C. The Chicago Blackhawks
D. The New York Rangers

8.11 What is the highest goals-to-assists differential by a player in a playoff career?

A. A differential of 18
B. A differential of 28
C. A differential of 38
D. A differential of 48

8.12 Which NHL great sawed his own leg cast off so that he could play in the Stanley Cup playoffs?

A. Bernie Geoffrion
B. Gordie Howe
C. Ted Lindsay
D. Stan Mikita

8.13 What was Philadelphia goalie Bernie Parent referring to when he said before Game 3 of the 1975 Stanley Cup finals: "I wouldn't take my boat out in these conditions"?

A. A low-lying fog on the ice
B. A rash of injuries plaguing his Flyer teammates

C. Plastic cups thrown on the ice by unhappy fans

D. Ice coolant seeping up through the rink surface from a broken pipe

8.14 **What is the greatest number of Cup-winning goals allowed by a goalie in a career?**

A. Two goals

B. Four goals

C. Six goals

D. Eight goals

8.15 **What is the greatest number of different NHL franchises a general manager has led to the Stanley Cup?**

A. Two franchises

B. Three franchises

C. Four franchises

D. Five franchises

8.16 **What is the greatest number of Stanley Cup losses by a team captain?**

A. Three Cup losses

B. Four Cup losses

C. Five Cup losses

D. Six Cup losses

8.17 **During the Stanley Cup playoffs two sets of caps and T-shirts are produced, each set declaring one finalist Cup champions. What happens to the merchandise for the team that doesn't win the Cup?**

A. It gets burned

B. It gets auctioned off

C. It goes to the losing team

D. It goes on sale at the Hockey Hall of Fame

Answers

8.1   C. 15 years.

Players who win a Stanley Cup early in their careers often say they never expected to wait so long for another chance to win it again. No one knows this better than the many rookies who claimed their first championship with Montreal in 1986. Brian Skrudland and Craig Ludwig waited 13 years, from 1986 to their next Cup with Dallas in 1999. Still, they didn't top Mickey MacKay, who won the Cup in 1915 with the Vancouver Millionaires and again 14 years later, in 1929, with the Boston Bruins. But another former Canadiens' Cup holder from 1986 established an even longer span between Cups. Chris Chelios won with Detroit in 2002, 15 years later.

8.2   C. The Minnesota Wild.

They were a team of cast-offs who shocked not one, but two, star-filled clubs into elimination reality. The Wild had a bunch of no-names but enough heart, character and audacity to come back from the brink twice facing 3–1 deficits to 4–3 series wins against Colorado in the first round followed by Vancouver in the second round during the 2003 playoffs. To say they did it with "the trap" would be unfair to coach Jacques Lemaire's mix-and-match line-up of muckers, grinders, role players and one budding superstar in Marian Gaborik. There were no fancy-pants skaters on this blue-collar team but in each game a different player stepped up, including goaltenders Dwayne Roloson and Manny Fernandez. Minnesota ran out of gas during the Conference Finals in a sweep by the Anaheim Mighty Ducks.

8.3   C. Mike Modano.

Looking for something special in hockey memorabilia? When

Modano went shopping on e-Bay he found his own 1999 Cup ring. Funny, he thought it was at DeBoulle Jewellers in Dallas, where he took it to get duplicated and upgraded. Apparently, the jeweler thought it was to be sold. He passed it on to a Florida man, who put the ring up for auction on e-Bay. Bidding on Modano's ring had hit us$20,000 before it was removed from the online site.

8.4 B. Jack Adams.

Adams's success and longevity earned him the distinction of winning the Stanley Cup in each of the NHL's first five decades. He won two Cups as a player, one with the Toronto Arenas in 1918 and another as a member of the old Ottawa Senators in 1927; two as coach of the Detroit Red Wings in 1936 and 1937; and seven as manager of the Red Wings in 1936, 1937, 1943, 1950, 1952, 1954 and 1955.

8.5 A. Three challenges.

If the original intentions of Lord Stanley were still being carried out as he had wished for his famous Cup, we might see a very different playoff format today. Rather than belonging to any one league, Stanley left specific instructions that his trophy was to be a challenge Cup. Under those guidelines, any beer league champions today could mount a challenge to get their names on the Stanley Cup. Not an appealing prospect for hockey fans, but it might make a great TV commercial. Nevertheless, since the NHL took control of the Cup in 1926, the league has had three formal challenges from non-NHL clubs: the 1931 Tulsa Oilers of the American Hockey Association, the 1932 Chicago Shamrocks of the AHA and the 1952 Cleveland Barons of the AHL. In each case, the NHL refused to meet in a showdown. Those serious considerations aside, another team, the Lethbridge Community College Kodiaks, issued a challenge to play for the Cup during the 1992 player's lockout.

8.6   **B. Toe Blake of the Montreal Canadiens.**
Surprisingly, only five captains in league history have scored
Stanley Cup winners. Bill Cook was the first in 1933 with New
York, followed by Toe Blake who netted two in 1944 and 1946,
Jean Béliveau with Montreal in 1965, Wayne Gretzky with
Edmonton in 1988 and Mark Messier for the Rangers in 1994.

8.7   **B. During the Montreal Canadiens' dynasty years of the
1950s.**
With the exclusion of substitute captain Serge Savard replacing injured captain Yvan Cournoyer during Montreal's Stanley
Cup run from 1976 to 1979, the last captain switch in consecutive Cup-winning years occurred when the Canadiens won
championships with retiring captain Butch Bouchard in 1956
and first-time captain Maurice Richard in 1957. Toronto also
changed team leaders in back-to-back Cup years, as captain Syl
Apps passed the torch to captain Ted Kennedy between Cup
wins in 1948 and 1949.

8.8   **D. Joe Sakic of the Colorado Avalanche.**
On May 1, 2004, Colorado's Joe Sakic made history and equaled
one of hockey's longest-standing playoff records, Maurice
Richard's legendary career mark of six overtime goals. Prior to
the 2004 playoffs, Sakic had four goals in overtime, tied with
several players but behind Glenn Anderson with five and
Richard, the record-holder with six. With his Avalanche facing
elimination, Sakic scored an overtime 1–0 winner to avert a
series sweep against the San Jose Sharks on April 28; and, in the
next game on May 1 he potted another overtime winner in a
2–1 victory to bring Colorado within one game of tying the
series. But the Sharks prevailed in Game 6 and turned back
Colorado's charge. Richard had held the record since he retired
in 1960 and, even though there are four playoff rounds today
compared to two in Richard's era, no one has eclipsed it.

8.9   D. Seven teams.

In the days when one third of NHL franchises had Canadian addresses and 16 clubs in the 21-team league qualified for post-season play, it wasn't unusual to see all or most of Canada's teams playoff bound. On two occasions—1982–83 and 1985–86—all seven Canadian teams earned a berth to the second season. In 1982–83, Edmonton and Montreal were the top teams north of the 49th parallel as Quebec, Calgary, Vancouver, Winnipeg and Toronto limped into the playoffs with .500 or worse records. In 1985–86, Edmonton and Calgary were one-two in the Smythe Division and Quebec and Montreal were one-two in the Adams, while Winnipeg, Vancouver and Toronto won first-round dates due to their divisional rankings despite finishing 16th, 17th and 18th overall.

8.10   B. The Boston Bruins.

Although their postseason rivalry dates back to the 1929 semifinals (with a 3–0 series win by Boston), Montreal's playoff hex over the Bruins began in earnest during the 1930 finals. In the regular season Boston dominated the NHL with a record .875 winning percentage and won all four meetings against the Canadiens. By the time the finals rolled around, the Bruins were already planning a parade route and their roster list for the Cup engravers. But then something happened to the team that had not lost back-to-back games all season. It was swept in consecutive games, 3–0 and 4–3, losing the Cup to Montreal in the best-of-three series. Boston's quick demise at the hands of the Canadiens prompted the NHL to extend the finals from a best-of-three to a best-of-five series.

8.11   C. A differential of 38.

Few players have ever matched Maurice Richard's intensity around the net. He lived to score goals. Between 1943 and 1960 he netted 82 and managed 44 assists, the differential of 38, the highest in playoff history.

Highest goals-to-assists differential, career*				
PLAYER	GP	GOALS	ASSISTS	DIF.
Maurice Richard	133	82	44	38
Dino Ciccarelli	141	73	45	28
Reggie Leach	94	47	22	25
Cam Neely	93	57	32	25

Current to 2003–04

8.12   A. Bernie Geoffrion.

Don't try this at home. It's not something any player would do today, but in Geoffrion's time there was a sixth straight Stanley Cup on the line. That was Doug Harvey and Bernie Geoffrion's logic when they hacked into Geoffrion's leg cast on a train ride to Chicago with their Canadiens, winners of five straight Cups, facing elimination, down 3–2 in the 1961 semi-finals against the Blackhawks. Geoffrion, who had torn ligaments in his left knee, picks up the story in his bio *Boom-Boom:* "Doug got a knife from the train kitchen and the two of us sneaked into the ladies' washroom. With my leg up on a chair, I watched my captain saw away at the heavy plaster of paris cast. He cut it lengthwise and the way the train was bouncing around, it was a miracle I wasn't cut. It seemed to take hours to complete the job. The next morning... Doug was feeling like a surgeon, 'I didn't do it in record time but you have to take into consideration the rolling train,' he said." Coach Toe Blake was furious but the Boomer's knee was frozen for the big game. He got to play sparingly on the power play with little reward. Montreal couldn't turn it around to become a six-time champion as Chicago went on to claim the Cup, its last since 1961.

8.13   A. A low-lying fog on the ice.

Who knows what caused it? High humidity, poor air circulation or angry hockey gods, it could have been any of the three. The result was a billowing broth that brought Game 3 of the Stanley Cup finals at Buffalo's Memorial Auditorium to a shuddering halt a dozen times on May 20, 1975. During the delays, the Philadelphia Flyers and Buffalo Sabres players skated in circles and rink attendants waved towels in an attempt to dissipate the mist. Buffalo finally won the game on Rene Robert's slap shot in overtime. Flyers goalie Bernie Parent could honestly claim he never saw it.

8.14   C. Six goals.
Glenn Hall was such a good goalie that three teams entrusted him despite his losing record in the finals. Hall lost with Detroit in 1956; Chicago in 1962 and 1965; and St. Louis in 1968, 1969 and 1970. His most famous playoff goal-against was his last Cup-loser to Boston's Bobby Orr. The goal produced hockey's most famous photograph, as Orr is sailing through the air, arms outstretched in celebration after being tripped up by St. Louis defender Noel Picard. Hall is seen picking himself up out of the net after being beaten by Orr. Hall did manage to get his name on one Cup, with Chicago in 1961.

8.15   C. Four franchises.
One of early hockey's most extraordinary and successful individuals, Tommy Gorman hasn't received his due among the pantheon of builders in NHL history. Icons such as Conn Smythe and Jack Adams never won as consistently with as many teams as Gorman. After turning Ottawa into the league's first dynasty (1920, 1921, 1923), he took over the New York Americans, then the Chicago Blackhawks (1934), the Montreal Maroons (1935) and the Montreal Canadiens (1944, 1946); seven Stanley Cups on four different franchises.

8.16   B. Four Cup losses.
Butch Bouchard holds the distinction of captaining more losing teams in the Stanley Cup finals than any other captain in

league history. Bouchard wore the C with the Montreal Canadiens for eight seasons from 1948–49 to 1955–56, winning two championships in 1953 and 1956, but losing another four to Toronto in 1951 and Detroit in 1952, 1954 and 1955.

8.17 A. It gets burned.
The NHL's consumer product division orders sets of hats and shirts for each finalist, but only one set of goods goes public, to the Cup champions when they skate around the ice with the Stanley Cup and celebrate in the dressing room. The Cup merchandise for the losing finalists gets incinerated at the manufacturer's plant. The NHL distributes some wrongfully labeled clothes to charity, but only in non-hockey playing countries.

Solutions to Games

Game 1: Hockey Crossword 1

```
 1      2      3      4      5      6          7
 M  I   G  H   T  Y   D  U   C  K   S          T
 I      E      O      I      O      8  9
                                    I   R  V   I   N
10      11
 N  I   L  A   N      C      R      12
                                    L   E
        13                                 14     15
 N      I   L  Y  A   K  O   V  A   L   C  H  U   K
                                    16
 E      N      A      I      O      I   C  E      E
17                    18             19
 S  W   A  R   M      E  D          N   H  L      N
                             20                21
 O      S      O             M  C   G   I  L   L
22  23   24     25                         26     27
 T  O    S      N  O   W      A     E      E  A   T
28                           29
 A  R   N  O   T  T           S  C  A   R      R  R
         30                              31
 E       P  E  T   R          I         J         O
32                     33      34
 M  T   K  E      A    I  N   T  H  E   N  E   T
         35  36     37            38
 L       L   O   W  E            E  R         T
39      40      41
 O  L   D       T  A   G  L   I   A  N  E   T  T  I
42               43
 R  Y   A   N           A         S      R      E
                44                45
 R      N   O  L   A   N          R   I  C  H  E   R
```

Game 2: Lefties & Righties

LEFTIES

1. Martin Brodeur	F. New Jersey Devils 2003
2. Glenn Hall	E. Chicago Blackhawks 1963
3. Turk Broda	A. Toronto Maple Leafs 1941
4. Ron Hextall	G. Philadelphia Flyers 1987
5. Terry Sawchuk	C. Detroit Red Wings 1955
6. Dominik Hasek	D. Buffalo Sabres 1999
7. Billy Smith	H. New York Islanders 1982
8. Patrick Roy	B. Montreal Canadiens 1992

RIGHTIES

1. Jose Theodore	H. Montreal Canadiens 2002
2. Chuck Gardiner	A. Chicago Blackhawks 1932
3. Grant Fuhr	G. Edmonton Oilers 1988
4. Bill Durnan	C. Montreal Canadiens 1944
5. Tom Barrasso	F. Buffalo Sabres 1984
6. Gilles Villemure	E. New York Rangers 1971
7. Dave Kerr	B. New York Rangers 1940
8. Tony Esposito	D. Chicago Blackhawks 1970

Game 3: Bench Boss Blues

On November 7, 1968, St. Louis' Red Berenson scored an NHL-record six goals in an 8–0 win on the road against the Philadelphia Flyers. In 1981 he was awarded the Jack Adams, as bench boss of those same Blues.

SUTTER

DEMERS

BURNS

SATHER

NOLAN

BOWMAN

LEMAIRE

RED BERENSON
ST LOUIS BLUES

Game 4: Magnetic Attractions

PART 1

1. Joe Nieuwendyk — D. Dallas 1999, New Jersey 2003
2. Terry Sawchuk — F. Detroit 1952, Toronto 1967
3. Mark Messier — E. Edmonton 1984, NY Rangers 1994
4. Ted Harris — G. Montreal 1965, Philadelphia 1975
5. Joe Kocur — A. NY Rangers 1994, Detroit 1998
6. Bryan Trottier — C. NY Islanders 1980, Pittsburgh 1991
7. Paul Coffey — B. Edmonton 1984, Pittsburgh 1991

PART 2

1. Patrick Roy — B. Montreal 1986, Colorado 1996
2. Brett Hull — E. Dallas 1999, Detroit 2002
3. Dick Duff — F. Toronto 1962, Montreal 1965
4. Larry Murphy — G. Pittsburgh 1992, Detroit 1997
5. Joe Mullen — D. Calgary 1989, Pittsburgh 1991
6. Frank Mahovlich — A. Toronto 1967, Montreal 1971
7. Chris Chelios — C. Montreal 1986, Detroit 2002

Game 5: Hockey Crossword 2

Game 6: Backup to the Greats

PART 1

1. Dominik Hasek/Detroit 2002	D. Manny Legace
2. Gump Worsley/Montreal 1966	E. Charlie Hodge
3. Mike Vernon/Calgary 1989	B. Bill Ranford
4. Bernie Parent/Philadelphia 1975	F. Wayne Stephenson
5. Ed Belfour/Dallas 1999	C. Roman Turek
6. Gerry Cheevers/Boston 1970	G. Eddie Johnston
7. Patrick Roy/Colorado 2001	A. David Aebischer

PART 2

1. Martin Brodeur/New Jersey 2003	E. Corey Schwab
2. Bill Ranford/Edmonton 1990	G. Grant Fuhr
3. Ken Dryden/Montreal 1978	F. Michel Larocque
4. Mike Richter/NY Rangers 1994	D. Glenn Healy
5. Johnny Bower/Toronto 1964	C. Don Simmons
6. Tom Barrasso/Pittsburgh 1992	A. Ken Wregget
7. Billy Smith/NY Islanders 1983	B. Roland Melanson

Game 7: Stanley Cup Captains

In descending order the 12 remaining letters spell out: **CHUCK GARDINER**, the only goalie to captain an NHL team to Stanley Cup greatness. Gardiner led the Chicago Blackhawks to the championship in 1934 while allowing a league-low 88 goals during the regular season. The Blackhawks were repeat Cup winners in 1938, again managing the lowest regular-season goal-count. Chicago's goalie that year was Mike Karakas.

Acknowledgements

Thanks to the following publishers and organizations for the use of quoted and statistical material:

· *The Hockey News*, various excerpts. Reprinted by permission of *The Hockey News*, a division of GTC *Transcontinental Publishing, Inc.*
· *The Official NHL Guide and Record Book*. Published by *Total Sports Canada*.
· *Total Hockey Second Edition* and *Total Stanley Cup* by Dan Diamond and Associates Inc. Published by *Total Sports* (1998, 2000).
· *The National Post*; *The Montreal Gazette*; *The Globe and Mail*; *The Edmonton Journal*; *Sports Illustrated*; *The Miami Herald*; and *The Associated Press*.

Care has been taken to trace ownership of copyright material contained in this book. The publishers welcome any information that will enable them to rectify any reference or credit in subsequent editions.

The author gratefully acknowledges the help of Jason Kay and everyone at *The Hockey News*; Gary Meagher and Benny Ercolani of the NHL; Phil Pritchard and Craig Campbell at the Hockey Hall of Fame; the staff at the McLellan-Redpath Library at McGill University; Rob Sanders, Susan Rana and Chris Labonte at Greystone Books; the many hockey writers, broadcast-journalists, media and Internet organizations who have made the game better through their own work; as well as statistical resources such as the Elias Sports Bureau, editor Christine Kondo, graphic artists Jessica Sullivan and Anastasia Efimova and puzzle designer Adrian van Vlaardingen for their dedication, expertise and creativity. Special thanks to Kerry Banks for additional hockey research.